ALSO BY TAYLOR BRANCH

The Cartel: Inside the Rise and Imminent Fall of the NCAA

The Clinton Tapes: Wrestling History with the President

At Canaan's Edge: America in the King Years, 1965–68

Pillar of Fire: America in the King Years, 1963–65

Parting the Waters: America in the King Years, 1954–63

Labyrinth (with Eugene M. Propper)

The Empire Blues

Second Wind (with Bill Russell)

Blowing the Whistle: Dissent in the Public Interest (with Charles Peters)

The King Years

Historic Moments
in the
Civil Rights Movement

Taylor Branch

SIMON & SCHUSTER PAPERBACKS
New York   London   Toronto   Sydney   New Delhi

Simon & Schuster Paperbacks
A Division of Simon & Schuster, Inc.
1230 Avenue of the Americas
New York, NY 10020

Parting the Waters copyright © 1988 by Taylor Branch
Pillar of Fire copyright © 1998 by Taylor Branch
At Canaan's Edge copyright © 2006 by Taylor Branch
Compilation and additional material copyright © 2013 by Taylor Branch

First Simon & Schuster paperback edition August 2013

SIMON & SCHUSTER PAPERBACKS and colophon are registered trademarks
of Simon & Schuster, Inc.

For information about special discounts for bulk purchases,
please contact Simon & Schuster Special Sales at
1-866-506-1949 or business@simonandschuster.com.

The Simon & Schuster Speakers Bureau can bring authors
to your live event. For more information or to book an event,
contact the Simon & Schuster Speakers Bureau at
1-866-248-3049 or visit our website at www.simonspeakers.com.

Designed by Joy O'Meara

Manufactured in the United States of America

10   9

The Library of Congress has cataloged the hardcover edition as follows:

Branch, Taylor.
    The King years : historic moments in the civil rights movement / by Taylor Branch.
— First Simon & Schuster hardcover edition.
        p. cm.
    1. African Americans—Civil rights. 2. Civil rights movements—United States—
History—20th century. 3. King, Martin Luther, Jr., 1929-1968. 4. United States—
History—1953-1961. 5. United States—History—1961-1969. I. Branch, Taylor.
Parting the waters. Selections. II. Branch, Taylor. Pillar of fire. Selections. III. Branch,
Taylor. At Canaan's edge. Selections. IV. Title.
E185.61.B7913 2013
  323.0973—dc23   2012006964
ISBN 978-1-4516-7897-0
ISBN 978-1-4516-6246-7 (pbk)
ISBN 978-1-4516-6247-4 (ebook)

Each of these titles has been previously published individually.

Photo credits can be found on p. 211.

For students of freedom and teachers of history

Contents

The King Years

Beyond state and local laws, which mandated racial separation everywhere from schools and businesses to public libraries, custom enforced segregation in houses of worship.

Preface

Since 1982, it took me twenty-four years and 2,306 pages to compile a three-book narrative history, *America in the King Years*, and the same enthrallment has distilled that work now into this slender volume. A singular wonder continues. I was not born or raised to care about politics, let alone to write history. The landmark *Brown* decision of 1954 had caught me a white first-grader in segregated Atlanta, Georgia, and my college graduation fourteen years later closely followed the King assassination. Through all the formative years in between, I remained fearfully oblivious to race until the relentless freedom movement redirected my entire life's interest. Permanent curiosity drove what would become a career ambition. As an outsider, I needed to learn what had sustained such resonant witness among near-peers of African descent.

Well before the 1988 publication of the first installment, *Parting the Waters*, I resolved to present my findings in storytelling form rather than the analytical synthesis common to history. No stylistic device can escape interpretation, and all history at bottom is an argument, but it seemed evident that cross-racial perspective has been especially vulnerable to distortion. Many standard histories taught, for instance, that the Civil War had little to do with slavery. President Kennedy recalled lessons at Harvard that Reconstruction trampled the rights of prominent white Southerners. Some textbooks still use an earnest, religious word—"Redeemers"—to describe the late-nineteenth-century politicians who imposed white supremacy and segregation, often by Klan-led terror. Clearly, over time, racial undercurrents have tilted and even inverted the prevailing view of our past.

This pitfall recommended a determined effort to ground cross-cultural history in fully human actors on all sides. Therefore, I resolved to avoid insofar as possible the distinctive labels of the civil rights era—"militant," "racist," "radical," "integrationist"—because such terms invite comfort and caricature rather than discovery. The goal was to pursue stories of impact until the clashing characters felt convincing by all available evidence, including their own lights.

My regimen made for a sprawling text and carried its own burdens of craft. *Parting the Waters* is dedicated to the late Septima Clark for a peculiar reason. Interviews with her left a strong personal effect on me, confirming what others from the civil rights movement felt, but she had functioned almost entirely "offstage" from the main historical narrative, as it were, teaching literacy and citizenship to rural sharecroppers. My dedication was a personal gesture of tribute mixed with regret, because I found it impossible within my storytelling rules to include Septima Clark in proportion to her influence.

Those same rules delayed my writing altogether at the outset, because they prohibited an introductory essay on the movement's incubator and laboratory, Southern black churches. Only luck turned up a potential solution in an unwritten trove of memory about Vernon Johns, Dr. King's predecessor at his church in Montgomery. The opening chapter presented this remarkable but unknown character on the calculated hope that his story itself could introduce the separate world of preachers and congregations, of warring politics and inspiration, from which the civil rights movement emerged.

Septima Clark and Vernon Johns are omitted from these pages along with many other figures I consider historically significant. Brevity offsets their absence. A hybrid framework for this volume seeks to preserve the authenticity of narrative detail within limited space. I have selected eighteen historical turning points from the 1954–68 era, described here in less than ten percent of the complete trilogy. Some are simple. Others are complex. They follow the spine of consequence through a transformative period that remains controversial. Each chapter begins with a short transitional summary, sometimes covering major events and intertwined plots with a paragraph or two. These new passages are necessarily compressed, interpretive, and open to argument, but they provide economical context so that readers can experience and absorb the key moments.

Those moved to seek fuller descriptions can find them in my books and many others, with voluminous reference notes. Our goal in this edition is to convey both the spirit and sweep of an extraordinary movement. Newer generations will find here the gist of a patriotic struggle in which the civil rights pioneers, like modern Founders, moved an inherited world of hierarchy and subjugation toward common citizenship. Others can recall vivid triumph and tragedy at the heart of national purpose for the United States, whose enduring story is freedom. The unvarnished history should resist fearful tides to diminish that story. Above all, the King years should serve as a bracing reminder that citizens and leaders can work miracles together despite every hardship, against great odds.

A community-wide assembly responds to oratory during the Montgomery Bus Boycott. Within the precarious sanctuary of black churches, such mass meetings grew into a distinctive tool of solidarity for the civil rights movement.

— CHAPTER ONE —

The Montgomery Bus Boycott: Martin Luther King's First Public Address, 1955

U.S. history has been marked and largely defined by political struggle over a "self-evident" truth asserted in the (1776) Declaration of Independence: that "all men are created equal." From the American Revolution forward, that founding principle has ignited controversy over the role of free government to secure "civil rights." The phrase, which pertains literally to anyone's rights of citizenship, acquired a strong racial connotation through chronic upheavals over slavery and segregation, lasting more than a century before and after the Civil War of 1861–65. Even today, the civil rights cause is associated in common parlance with Americans of African descent.

An intense phase of this history, known as the modern civil rights movement, coincided with the short public career of its signature leader, Dr. Martin Luther King, Jr. (1954–68). The effects have rippled far and deep, from freedom abroad to cultural identities at home. The chief instigators referred to themselves first as Negroes, then black people, and subsequently African Americans. Prominent among catalyzing events came the Supreme Court's landmark *Brown v. Board of Education* decision on May 17, 1954. "Separate educational facilities are inherently unequal," wrote Chief Justice Earl Warren, and a unanimous Court struck down as unconstitutional the school segregation laws of twenty states from Florida to Kansas.

The political earth shook, but then again it did not. Very little changed. A year later, two men kidnapped and lynched fourteen-year-old Emmett Till in rural Mississippi, allegedly for whistling at a white woman. Till's mother insisted that her son's bloated, mutilated corpse, when pulled from the Tallahatchie River, be displayed in an open casket "for all the world to see," and a sensationally segregated trial promptly acquitted two defendants who all but boasted of committing their crime to enforce the racial caste code. The Till case revealed a gaping chasm between real life and the Supreme Court's arid pronouncement of equality in law.

No one predicted the next spark. It was novel in venue, method, and cast, with a female protagonist. Other Negroes had been arrested off the segregated public buses of Montgomery, Alabama, for refusing orders to surrender seats to white people, but none had the galvanizing effect of the soft-spoken, determined seamstress Rosa Parks. On Thursday evening, December 1, 1955, word of her arrest spread by mouth, leaflet, and emergency conclave, amplified from Negro church pulpits that

Sunday. On Monday, stunned that ninety percent of Negro passengers boycotted the buses, an ad hoc protest committee chose a well-educated newcomer in town to address an assembly on what to do next.

[From *Parting the Waters*, pp. 137–42]

King raced home to his wife and new baby sometime after six. Hesitantly, he informed Coretta that he had been drafted as president of the new protest committee. Much to his relief, she did not object to the *fait accompli* and in fact said quietly that she would support him in whatever he did. King said he would have no time for supper. He had to leave for the mass meeting within half an hour, and after that he had to address a banquet sponsored by the YMCA, one of the only integrated organizations in Montgomery. Most on his mind was the speech at Holt Street—his first appearance as the new protest leader, the first words most of the audience would have heard from him. He went into his study and closed the door, wondering how he could possibly create such an important speech in a few minutes, when he required fifteen hours to prepare an ordinary sermon. His mind raced. He knew from his conscience that he wanted to answer one peevish charge that had appeared in both newspaper articles thus far—that the Negroes had borrowed the boycott tactic from the White Citizens Councils, which had openly adopted a policy of harsh economic reprisal against Negroes who fought segregation. King searched for the correct words by which he might distinguish the bus boycott from un-Christian coercion. He had written only a few notes on a piece of paper when it was time to go.

Elliott Finley, King's Morehouse friend with the pool table, drove him to the rally. King had a few minutes to think in the car. A traffic jam on the way to Holt Street extended the time a bit, and then a bit more, until they realized they could go no farther—the church was surrounded. The hostile press later estimated the crowd at five thousand people; Negroes put it at two or three times that figure. Whatever the exact number, only a small fraction of the bodies fit inside the church, and loudspeakers were being set up to amplify the proceedings to an outdoor crowd that stretched over several acres, across streets and around cars that had been parked at all angles. The prominent local patrons Clifford and Virginia Durr never got within three blocks of the church door. The missionary Lutheran pastor Robert Graetz was the only white supporter inside—the only white face seen there other than reporters and cameramen. "You know something, Finley," said King, as he prepared to abandon the car. "This could turn into something big." It took him fifteen minutes to push his way through the crowd. Shortly thereafter, the Holt Street pastor called him to the pulpit.

King stood silently for a moment. When he greeted the enormous crowd of strangers, who were packed in the balconies and aisles, peering in through the windows and upward from seats on the floor, he spoke in a deep voice, stressing his diction in a slow introductory cadence. "We are here this evening—for serious business," he said, in even pulses, rising and then falling in pitch. When he paused, only one or two "yes" responses came up from the crowd, and they were quiet ones. It was a throng of shouters, he could see, but they were waiting to see where he would take them. "We are here in a general sense, because first and foremost—we are American citizens—and we are determined to apply our citizenship—to the fullness of its means," he said. "But we are here in a specific sense—because of the bus situation in Montgomery." A general murmur of assent came back to him, and the pitch of King's voice rose gradually through short, quickened sentences. "The situation is not at all new. The problem has existed over endless years. Just the other day—just last Thursday to be exact—one of the finest citizens in Montgomery—not one of the finest Negro citizens—but one of the finest citizens in Montgomery—was taken from a bus—and carried to jail and arrested—because she refused to give up—to give her seat to a white person."

The crowd punctuated each pause with scattered "Yeses" and "Amens." They were with him in rhythm, but lagged slightly behind in enthusiasm. Then King spoke of the law, saying that the arrest was doubtful even under the segregation ordinances, because reserved Negro and white bus sections were not specified in them. "The law has never been clarified at that point," he said, drawing an emphatic "Hell, no" from one man in his audience. "And I think I speak with—with legal authority—not that I have any legal authority—but I think I speak with legal authority behind me—that the law—the ordinance—the city ordinance has never been totally clarified." This sentence marked King as a speaker who took care with distinctions, but it took the crowd nowhere. King returned to the special nature of Rosa Parks. "And since it had to happen, I'm happy it happened to a person like Mrs. Parks," he said, "for nobody can doubt the boundless outreach of her integrity. Nobody can doubt the height of her character, nobody can doubt the depth of her Christian commitment." That's right, a soft chorus answered. "And just because she refused to get up, she was arrested," King repeated. The crowd was stirring now, following King at the speed of a medium walk.

He paused slightly longer. "And you know, my friends, there comes a time," he cried, "when people get tired of being trampled over by the iron feet of oppression." A flock of "Yeses" was coming back at him when suddenly the individual responses dissolved into a rising cheer and applause exploded beneath the cheer—all within the space of a second. The startling noise rolled on and on, like a wave that refused to break, and just when it seemed that the roar must finally weaken, a wall of sound came in from the enormous crowd outdoors to push the volume still higher. Thunder seemed to be added to the lower register—the sound of feet stomping on the wooden floor—until the loudness became something that was not so much heard as it was sensed by vibrations in the lungs. The giant cloud of noise shook the building and refused to go away. One sentence had set it loose somehow, pushing the call-and-response of the Negro church service past the din of a political rally and on to something else that King had never known before....

Perhaps daunted by the power that was bursting forth from the crowd, King moved quickly to address the pitfalls of a boycott. "Now let us say that we are not here advocating violence," he said. "We have overcome that." A man in the crowd shouted, "Repeat that! Repeat that!" "I want it to be known throughout Montgomery and throughout this nation that we are Christian people," said King, putting three distinct syllables in "Christian." "The only weapon that we have in our hands this evening is the weapon of protest." There was a crisp shout of approval right on the beat of King's pause. He and the audience moved into a slow trot. "If we were incarcerated behind the iron curtains of a communistic nation—we couldn't do this. If we were trapped in the dungeon of a totalitarian regime—we couldn't do this. But the great glory of American democracy is the right to protest for right." When the shouts of approval died down, King rose up with his final reason to avoid violence, which was to distinguish themselves from their opponents in the Klan and the White Citizens Council. "There will be no crosses burned at any bus stops in Montgomery," he said. "There will be no white persons pulled out of their homes and taken out on some distant road and murdered. There will be nobody among us who will stand up and defy the Constitution of this nation."

King paused. The church was quiet but it was humming. "My friends," he said slowly, "I want it to be known—that we're going to work with grim and bold determination—to gain justice on the buses in this city. And we are not wrong. We are not wrong in what we are doing." There was a muffled shout of anticipation, as the crowd sensed that King was moving closer to the heart of his cause. "If we are wrong—the Supreme Court of this nation is wrong," King sang out. He was rocking now, his voice seeming to be at once deep and high-pitched. "If we are wrong—God Almighty is wrong!" he shouted, and the crowd seemed to explode a second time, as it had done when he said they were tired. Wave after wave of noise broke over them, cresting into the farthest reaches of the ceiling. They were far beyond Rosa Parks or the bus laws. King's last cry had fused blasphemy to the edge of his faith and the heart of theirs. The noise swelled until King cut through it to move past a point of unbearable tension. "If we are wrong—Jesus of Nazareth was merely a utopian dreamer and never came down to earth!

If we are wrong—justice is a lie." This was too much. He had to wait some time before delivering his soaring conclusion, in a flight of anger mixed with rapture: "And we are determined here in Montgomery—to work and fight until justice runs down like water, and righteousness like a mighty stream!" The audience all but smothered this passage from Amos, the lowly herdsman prophet of Israel who, along with the priestly Isaiah, was King's favorite biblical authority on justice.

He backed off the emotion to speak of the need for unity, the dignity of protest, the historical precedent of the labor movement. Comparatively speaking, his subject matter was mundane, but the crowd stayed with him even through paraphrases of abstruse points from theologian Reinhold Niebuhr. "And I want to tell you this evening that it is not enough for us to talk about love," he said. "Love is one of the pinnacle parts of the Christian faith. There is another side called justice. And justice is really love in calculation. Justice is love correcting that which would work against love." He said that God was not just the God of love: "He's also the God that standeth before the nations and says, 'Be still and know that I am God—and if you don't obey Me I'm gonna break the backbone of your power—and cast you out of the arms of your international and national relationships.'" Shouts and claps continued at a steady rhythm as King's audacity overflowed. "Standing beside love is always justice," he said. "Not only are we using the tools of persuasion—but we've got to use the tools of coercion." He called again for unity. For working together. He appealed to history, summoning his listeners to behave so that sages of the future would look back at the Negroes of Montgomery and say they were "a people who had the moral courage to stand up for their rights." He said they could do that. "God grant that we will do it before it's too late." Someone said, "Oh, yes." And King said, "As we proceed with our program—let us think on these things."

The crowd retreated into stunned silence as he stepped away from the pulpit. The ending was so abrupt, so anticlimactic. The crowd had been waiting for him to reach for the heights a third time at his conclusion, following the rules of oratory. A few seconds passed before memory and spirit overtook disappointment. The applause continued as King made his way out of the church, with people reaching to touch him. Members from

King's own church marveled, having never seen him let loose like that. Rev. Ralph Abernathy remained behind, reading negotiating demands from the pulpit. The boycott was on. King would work on his timing, but his oratory had just made him forever a public person. In the few short minutes of his first political address, a power of communion emerged from him that would speak inexorably to strangers who would both love and revile him, like all prophets. He was twenty-six, and had not quite twelve years and four months to live.

Sit-in demonstrators John Salter, Joan Trumpauer, and Anne Moody (*left to right*) endure persecution at a lunch counter.

— CHAPTER TWO —

Sit-ins and the Student Nonviolent Coordinating Committee (SNCC), 1960

The Montgomery boycott endured persecutions all through 1956, until the U.S. Supreme Court dissolved bus segregation there by explicit order in December. Nationally, this limited victory faded into a quaint story of humble Negroes protesting with tired feet. King's own New York publisher presented him as a voice apart in the cover line for his first book, *Stride Toward Freedom*: "A Leader of His People Tells the Montgomery Story."

One magazine estimated generously that King traveled 780,000 miles a year in the late 1950s, preaching against segregation. Discreetly, he consulted Billy Graham about how the celebrated evangelist's "crusade" model might convert the white South from segregation, city by city. Beneath public radar, he addressed a "Prayer Pilgrimage" for the Negro vote on the Washington Mall in 1957, and flew to Ghana for the first of colonial Africa's hopeful independence ceremonies ahead. The next year, he survived the near-fatal stabbing by a deranged woman in Harlem. King visited India in 1959 to find puzzling splits among the heirs of the nonviolent pioneer Mahatma Gandhi, including Prime Minister Jawaharlal Nehru, who was developing nuclear weapons to deter India's national enemy, Pakistan.

Meanwhile, reluctantly but decisively, President Dwight D. Eisenhower dispatched the 101st Airborne Division for a year to enforce court-ordered integration by the first nine Negro students at Little Rock's Central High School. Weeks later, in October 1957, the Soviet Union launched Sputnik, the world's first space satellite, which shocked the United States into sustained national improvements in rocketry, science education, and even a new interstate highway system.

This international Cold War dominated the headlines. Trailing far beneath, isolated pilgrims experimented in freedom across the color line. Southern idealists dared to meet at church camps or the YMCA, and Rev. James Lawson, a Korean War resister, trained a small workshop of Nashville students in nonviolent discipline. Hidden networks for change percolated within the conformist image of the 1950s. Dr. King chafed that his gift of oratory alone could not move entrenched segregation. Then on February 1, 1960, as he moved home to copastor his father's church in Atlanta, an unlikely movement sparked in Greensboro, North Carolina.

[From *Parting the Waters*, pp. 272–91]

No one had time to wonder why the Greensboro sit-in was so different. In the previous three years, similar demonstrations had occurred in at least sixteen other cities. Few of them made the news, all faded quickly from public notice, and none had the slightest catalytic effect anywhere else. By contrast, Greensboro helped define the new decade. Almost certainly, the lack of planning helped create the initial euphoria. Because the four students at Woolworth's had no plan, they began with no self-imposed limitations. They defined no tactical goals. They did not train or drill in preparation. They did not dwell on the many forces that might be used against them. Above all, they did not anticipate that Woolworth's white managers would—instead of threatening to have them arrested—flounder in confusion and embarrassment. The surprise discovery of defensiveness within the segregated white world turned their fear into elation.

The spontaneity and open-endedness of the first Greensboro sit-in flashed through the network of activists who had been groping toward the same goal. On the first night, the first four protesters themselves contacted Floyd McKissick, who, as a maverick lawyer and NAACP Youth Council leader, had joined Rev. Douglas Moore in the Durham ice cream parlor case and other small sit-ins. McKissick and Moore rushed to nearby Greensboro. Simultaneously, the news traveled along parallel lines of communication with such speed that a vice president of the mostly white National Student Association was in Greensboro on February 2, the second day, before any word of the sit-in had appeared in the public media.

On the third day, when the number of protesters passed eighty, Douglas Moore called James Lawson in Nashville with a volley of bulletins. The protest would continue to grow, he reported, as enthusiastic student volunteers were only too eager to absorb the organizing discipline of the adults who had arrived to work in the background. The sit-in "command center" at North Carolina A&T was operating with crisp, military efficiency—briefing new protesters on nonviolence, quashing rumors, dispatching fresh troops as needed. Most important, Moore reported, sympathetic sit-ins were about to begin in Durham, Raleigh, and other North Carolina cities.

Moore, who knew already that Lawson had been preparing for new Nashville protests, urged him to speed up the schedule so that the movement could spread into other states. Lawson promised to try. Moore then made other calls, including one to Glenn Smiley of the nonviolent peace activist group FOR (Fellowship of Reconciliation). McKissick called Gordon Carey from the Congress of Racial Equality (CORE), who had worked on Wyatt Walker's Richmond march and the Miami sit-ins the previous year. Carey flew from New York to Durham at the end of the first week. By Saturday, the Greensboro sit-in counted some four hundred students, and Kress, the other big downtown dime store, had been added to the target list. A bomb scare that day interrupted the demonstrations. Later, Klansmen and youth-gang members crowded inside the stores to menace the protesters. Store managers who had been desperately polite all week now threatened to call in legal force.

Before serious reprisal fell upon Greensboro, fresh sit-ins broke out the following Monday in the surrounding North Carolina cities of Raleigh, Durham, and Winston-Salem. Three days later in nearby High Point, students assembled at a church before marching downtown to the segregated lunch counters, and as it happened, King's colleague Rev. Fred Shuttlesworth had come in from Birmingham to preach the midweek service for the minister of that church. Shuttlesworth became the first eyewitness from the tough Deep South states below North Carolina. He saw the well-dressed students step off in good order, like soldiers in the joyous early stages of a popular war, and he heard that it was the same in the other North Carolina towns—only bigger. Shuttlesworth promptly called Ella Baker at King's office in Atlanta. He was not the first to report to her about the sit-ins, but he was the first voice of authority from the inner circle of the Southern Christian Leadership Conference (SCLC) preachers. This is it, he told Baker. "You must tell Martin that we must get with this," said Shuttlesworth, adding that the sit-ins might "shake up the world."

The movement first leaped across state lines on the day after the High Point sit-in. An SCLC preacher in Rock Hill, South Carolina, reported by phone to McKissick that his charges were "ready to go." They went from his church to the lunch counters on Friday, the same day police arrested forty-one students sitting in at the Cameron Village Woolworth store in Raleigh. In handcuffs, the Raleigh students swept across the threshold of the jail with eyes closed and hearts pounding, and, like the bus boycotters four years earlier, they soon re-emerged on bail to discover that their identities had not been crushed. They were unharmed and did not feel like trash. A flood of relief swelled their enthusiasm.

In Nashville that Friday night, Lawson presided over what turned out to be the first mass meeting of the sit-in movement. About five hundred new volunteers crowded into the First Baptist Church along with the seventy-five veterans of the nonviolence workshop. Lawson and the other adults argued for delay, on the grounds that only a small fraction of the students had received any training. This was not a game, they said. Sooner or later the city would put demonstrators in jail, and their organization—the Nashville Christian Leadership Conference, a local affiliate of King's SCLC—had less than $100 in reserve. They needed time to raise a bail fund. These and other words of caution gave way to a tide of student sentiment, however, and Lawson found himself giving a crash course on nonviolence late into the night. He told the crowd how to behave in the face of a hundred possible emergencies, how to avoid violating the loitering laws, how to move to and from the lunch counters in orderly shifts, how to fill the seats of students who needed to go to the bathroom, even how to dress: stockings and heels for the women, coats and ties for the fellows. When in doubt, he stressed, the newcomers should take their cue from the behavior of the workshop members who had demonstrated before.

They broke up that night amid nervous prayers and whispers of "Good luck," and Lawson's logistical plan worked smoothly the next morning. Church cars traveled a circuit between the First Baptist Church and designated pickup spots near Nashville's four Negro colleges—Fisk University, Tennessee State, Meharry Medical, and the Baptist seminary. When all were assembled at the First Baptist staging area, Lawson moved them out five hundred strong. White Nashville, which had changed hands nearly a dozen times during the Civil War, awoke slowly to a kind of invasion force it never had encountered before, as rows of neatly dressed Negro college students filed into the downtown stores to wait for food service.

The Nashville students—destined to establish themselves as the largest, most disciplined, and most persistent of the nonviolent action groups in the South—extended the sit-in movement into its third state. Their success helped form the model of the student group—recruited from the campuses, quartered in the churches, and advised by preachers. Elated with the early results, Lawson called King, Ella Baker, and Douglas Moore, among others, to exchange reports. Each of them in turn called acquaintances who might help open other fronts. By the end of February, sit-in campaigns were under way in thirty-one Southern cities across eight states. News attention remained scanty for the most part in both white and Negro media, largely because people were conditioned to think of student antics as transient events. Moore predicted that the sit-ins soon would put an end to such complacency. "If Woolworth and the other stores think this is just another panty raid," he told reporters, "they haven't had their sociologists in the field recently.". . .

King embraced the students for taking the step he had been toying with for the past three years—of *seeking out* a nonviolent confrontation with the segregation laws. He had traveled halfway around the world to wrestle with obscure Gandhian conundrums, and declared countless times that he was prepared to die for his beliefs, but he had never been quite willing to follow his thoughts outside the relative safety of oratory. With a simple, schoolboyish deed, the students cut through all the complex knots he had been trying to untie at the erudite Institutes on Nonviolence. His generosity of spirit made it easy for him to give the students credit for their inspiration, and his own lingering fears no doubt added to his admiration of their courage. Even now, King himself was not ready to join them at a lunch counter or otherwise force a test of the segregation laws with his person. He made no pledge to do so at Durham, but the pull of it fueled his exhortations to the assembled students. "Let us not fear going to jail," he declared. "If the officials threaten to arrest us for standing up for our rights, we must answer by saying that we are willing and prepared to fill up the jails of the South. . . . And so I would urge you to continue your struggle." "Fill up the jails" was a new battle cry for King, an incendiary one by the standards of both races. . . .

Emotions in Montgomery ran high that Saturday [February 27], the day of the first mass arrests in Nashville. Rumors of student sit-ins at Montgomery's downtown lunch counters attracted roving bands of angry white people armed with small baseball bats. There were no sit-ins, but exchanges between the white vigilantes and ordinary Negro shoppers occasionally flashed into violence. While one white man scuffled with a Negro woman on the sidewalk, his companion bludgeoned her from the blind side. There was little doubt about the nature of the encounter or the names of the people involved, because Sunday's *Advertiser* carried a photograph with a caption naming the attacker. The white photographer and reporter at the scene both said that the police had stood by passively, and that the crack of the baseball bat on the woman's head could be heard from half a block away. Alabama Governor John Patterson announced that he would leave the investigation to local officials. Police Commissioner L. B. Sullivan—who had replaced Clyde Sellers since the bus boycott—blamed the Negro students for causing the original disturbance and the *Advertiser* for publishing the photograph. Editor Grover Hall, while dividing the larger blame between "rash, misled young Negroes" and "white thugs," defended his newspaper against the police commissioner. "Sullivan's problem is not a photographer with a camera," he wrote. "Sullivan's problem is a white man with a baseball bat." . . .

At Orangeburg, South Carolina . . . some four hundred students from South Carolina State and Claflin College marched downtown to sit at the segregated lunch counters. Forewarned, local police and units of special state agents intercepted them with massed force, firing tear gas and water hoses before they arrested 388 of the student marchers. Doused, choking students, herded into an enclosed park, found themselves as stunned by their own calm as by the ferocity of the police rebuff. Charles McDew, leader of the Orangeburg march, would always recall looking back at the melee from a police car after his arrest, to see one of the hulking local football stars, David "Deacon" Jones, holding in his arms a crippled female student who had been knocked down by the firehoses. The expression on Jones's face was one of peaceful sadness instead of rage. The sight of it haunted McDew. Although he had little use for nonviolence or even for

Christianity, he became convinced that an inescapable power could be buried in doctrines of meekness and humanity.

Orangeburg was the first of some forty new cities that experienced student demonstrations in March, as the sit-in movement spread into Georgia, West Virginia, Texas, and Arkansas. . . . Nearly a hundred students from nineteen states spent the first weekend of April at Highlander Folk School, the South's embattled retreat for interracial discussion, where they exchanged phone numbers, philosophies, and their favorite tips about how to run a demonstration. A quartet led by the flamboyant Nashville Seminary student James Bevel performed "You Better Leave Segregation Alone" and other original compositions in close harmony "do-wop" style, drawing great enthusiasm from the audience. The students were suffused with energy, frankly amazed by their introduction to one another and to Highlander. Guy Carawan, Highlander's resident folksinger, taught them old songs that had evolved through the 1930s labor movement into the Highlander repertoire: "We Shall Not Be Moved," "Keep Your Eyes on the Prize," "This Little Light of Mine," "I'm Gonna Sit at the Welcome Table," and "We Shall Overcome."

All this was new, and the spirit of discovery ran so strong that many of the same students journeyed to North Carolina less than two weeks later for a second conference, organized by Ella Baker. She persuaded King to guarantee the expenses with $800. . . . With Glenn Smiley and Douglas Moore, Baker made the arrangements with her own alma mater, Shaw University in Raleigh. The trio agreed that James Lawson would serve as "dean" of the conference, with Moore as his assistant.

On April 15, nearly 150 students from nine states poured into North Carolina, where the first sit-ins had erupted ten weeks earlier. Very few of them had heard of Lawson, but his keynote address on the first night created a mass of instant disciples. He spoke in a manner as learned and idealistic as King's. "Love is the central motif of nonviolence," he declared. "Love is the force by which God binds man to Himself and man to man. Such love goes to the extreme; it remains loving and forgiving even in the midst of hostility. It matches the capacity of evil to inflict suffering with an even more enduring capacity to absorb evil, all the while persisting in love." In the same speech, however, Lawson balanced these lofty statements with trenchant realism. "Most of us will be grandparents before we can lead normal lives," he said. He directed withering criticism at the NAACP as "too conservative," charging that the NAACP journal *The Crisis* was no more than "the magazine of the black bourgeoisie." Lawson denounced the NAACP for its preoccupation with fund-raising and lawsuits. Such a strategy unjustly and unwisely exposed the courts to disrepute, Lawson insisted, by heaping upon them tasks that were inherently political. He attacked the NAACP for begging, for failing to develop what he called "our greatest resource: a people no longer the victims of racial evil, who can act in a disciplined manner to implement the Constitution."

This was strong stuff. Lawson lifted the taboo against NAACP criticism much more directly than did King, who was content to praise the students for "moving away from tactics which are suitable merely for gradual and long-term change." Like Lawson, King swept away the crowd with his speech. He remained the conference's celebrity, but Lawson's frankness carried the appeal of revealed secrets. Many of the students adopted Lawson as their own private discovery. Together, the two leaders inspired an enthusiasm for nonviolent activism such as neither had ever seen. It was the defining, animating zeal of the conference, so readily accepted that the students put the word "Nonviolent" into the name they chose for themselves: Student Nonviolent Coordinating Committee. They were the first civil rights group ever to do so.

May 14, 1961, outside Anniston, Alabama, a white mob attacked and burned this Greyhound bus carrying the pioneer load of interracial Freedom Riders.

— CHAPTER THREE —

Freedom Rides I:
The Nashville Initiative, 1961

Student sit-ins continued throughout 1960, concentrated in Southern cities with predominantly Negro colleges. Not until October 19, 1960, over his father's objections, did King accept persistent invitations to join Atlanta students protesting a segregated lunch counter at the prestigious

Rich's Department Store. It was King's fourth arrest since the bus boycott had begun—the first in which he deliberately sought to be jailed.

The incarceration of Martin Luther King touched off furtive political maneuvering in the final stages of the 1960 presidential campaign. Vice President Richard Nixon, the Republican nominee, stressed the GOP's century-old bond between Negro voters and the party of Abraham Lincoln, but did not specifically mention King's plight. Nixon's opponent, Senator John F. Kennedy, while cultivating his essential Democratic base in the white "solid South," did place a sympathetic phone call to King's wife, Coretta. Political experts, including Nixon in defeat, later isolated Kennedy's gesture as the cause of a razor-thin victory. The "miracle" phone call elevated King in national politics. He became the Negro whose name determined a president.

In 1961, President Kennedy took office with a youthful pledge of leadership toward a "New Frontier." After his disastrous clandestine invasion at Cuba's Bay of Pigs, Kennedy boldly announced a national goal to land on the moon by 1969. That same spring, the civil rights group CORE (Congress of Racial Equality) sent thirteen trained volunteers on a Freedom Ride through the South, testing the Supreme Court's recent guarantee of the right to integrated travel on interstate buses.

On Sunday, May 14, 1961, a white mob attacked and burned one bus of Freedom Riders outside Anniston, Alabama. Minutes later, a Ku Klux Klan posse severely beat the second busload on arrival at the Trailways station in Birmingham. Attorney General Robert Kennedy sent officials to evacuate the battered CORE riders, amid sensational publicity, but students from Nashville's nonviolent workshop already had suspended a Mother's Day picnic. Their response to the distant crisis would enlarge both the scope and identity of the civil rights movement.

[From *Parting the Waters*, pp. 428–47]

In Nashville, where a revolving mass of sit-in veterans had been debating the Freedom Ride almost continuously for twenty-four hours, the discussion shifted when they got word that the CORE group was abandoning the buses. Suddenly, the issue was not one of reinforcing the riders but replacing them, not boosting the ride's success but preventing its failure. Fisk University student Diane Nash soon traced CORE executive James Farmer to Washington, where he was attending his father's funeral. She asked him whether CORE would object if Nashville students went to Birmingham and took up where the original riders left off. Her request left Farmer temporarily speechless, but he gave his consent. . . .

[M]addening details consumed all of Tuesday, May 16. The smallest questions of logistics—should they ride segregated from Nashville to Birmingham, or should they stick to their principles at the risk of being stopped even before they could begin to take up the Freedom Ride?—opened large questions of philosophy and personal belief, and just when one issue seemed to be settled someone would confess an old doubt or a new fear. Phone calls from . . . sobbing or angry parents who had just seen gruesome news footage of wounded rider Jim Peck disembarking from the plane in New Orleans destabilized the emotions beneath a wobbly consensus. That evening, with the divided Nashville adults agreeing to donate $900 from the sit-in treasury without explicitly endorsing the student plan, Diane Nash pushed ahead with a call of final notice to Shuttlesworth. "The students," she told him, "have decided that we can't let violence overcome. We are going to come into Birmingham to continue the Freedom Ride."

"Young lady," Shuttlesworth replied in his most authoritative voice, "do you know that the Freedom Riders were almost killed here?"

"Yes," Nash said tersely. Her patience was almost spent. "That's exactly why the ride must not be stopped. If they stop us with violence, the movement is dead. We're coming. We just want to know if you can meet us.". . .

Monday's siege at the Birmingham Greyhound terminal was essentially re-created on Wednesday. Police commanders, straddling the thin edge between protection and repression, between maintaining peace and preserving segregation, now emphasized to the Freedom Riders that the police, as they could see, were protecting them from a mob of angry white people. It would make their task much easier, they advised, if the Freedom Riders would not mingle interracially there in the white waiting room. To this argument, and to a host of similar blandishments, the Freedom Riders steadfastly replied that they intended to wait there in accordance with the Supreme Court's *Boynton* decision and to catch the five o'clock bus to Montgomery.

The stalemate lasted three more hours, during which time some of the crowd's hostility was redirected toward the officers who were constantly pushing them back. Finally, police commissioner Eugene "Bull" Connor himself appeared at the terminal, and as the Freedom Riders moved to board the Montgomery bus he ordered his men to arrest them. Cheers went up from the bystanders as the police officers handcuffed the ten riders and dragged them to the transport vans. When Connor's nemesis, Fred Shuttlesworth, demanded to know why this was being done, he too was arrested, which drew more cheers. Connor, having satisfied the segregationists by deed, now moved to placate the image-conscious city fathers by telling reporters that he was placing the Freedom Riders under "protective custody." The students sang freedom songs as they were transported to the Birmingham jail. They tried to calm themselves by saying that this was no worse than another night on the Nashville picket line. . . .

Early [Thursday] morning, unannounced and unrecorded by the official schedule, Robert Kennedy walked into the White House and up to the President's private quarters, accompanied by his top assistants Byron White and Burke Marshall. The trio from Justice caught the President in his pajamas, with his breakfast sitting in front of him. The Attorney General greeted his brother as though they were resuming an interrupted business meeting. "As you know, the situation is getting worse in Alabama," he began. The new batch of Freedom Riders were refusing to eat in the Birmingham jail, demanding to be put back on the bus. Greyhound officials, upset about their firebombed bus, were refusing to transport any Freedom Riders without guarantees of police protection, and Governor Patterson was refusing to repeat the guarantee he had made and then half-repudiated on Monday. In fact, the governor was hedging and equivocating—almost hiding, Kennedy reported—for fear of being caught in a political trap. If Patterson declared that he would protect the Freedom Riders as interstate travelers, then Alabama voters might say that he had knuckled under to the federal government, sacrificed Alabama's segregation laws, and accepted the unmanly role of nursemaid to the hated group of interracial trouble-makers. If, on the other hand, Patterson declared he could not or would not protect the Freedom Riders, he would be admitting limits to state sover-eignty and all but inviting the federal government to assume police power in his state. To Patterson, either course was political suicide.

The result thus far was a stalemate, which was the outcome least toler-able to the federal government. The Attorney General did not say—he did not have to—that his own highly visible role in getting the first Freedom Riders out of Birmingham had helped elevate the drama into a major national story, with reporters still waiting in Alabama for the federal gov-ernment to resolve this second crisis. For Robert Kennedy, the dilemma already was a humbling demonstration of the race issue's mystifying, unconventional powers. A handful of faceless, nameless, half-suicidal pacifists had seized his attention by the simple act of riding a bus. Less than two weeks after Kennedy's sweeping rhetorical commitment to ac-tivist law enforcement in civil rights—"We will move"—reality contrived for him a cruel test in which the Administration's reputation hung on whether he could empower a single bus to move out of the Birmingham station. . . .

President Kennedy asked only a few questions, mostly about timing. For his own unstated reasons, he asked Marshall whether it was likely he could get by without making a decision until Monday. Marshall replied that the stalemate probably would not hold that long. The Freedom Riders were being held illegally, without charges, and lawyers were demanding their release. The President, switching to the preferred way out, wondered how they could move most effectively to induce Governor Patterson to take responsibility. He knew Patterson personally. Was it time for direct contact by him? If so, should it be by telephone, telegram, or letter? It was decided to place a call to Patterson's office in Montgomery. Moments later a chagrined operator reported that the governor was said to be on a fishing boat somewhere far out in the Gulf of Mexico. Patterson was unavailable even to the White House. This egregious snubbing of the President introduced the Kennedys to a far different John Patterson from the one they had known.

There was to be no word of the President's involvement. The Attorney General would say only that he was meeting with his own advisers in an effort to maintain law and order in Alabama, and the three Justice Department men would push forward with the contingencies outlined that morning. With these orders understood, the President excused himself to dress for the day. Burke Marshall, looking back into the room as he made his exit, was struck by the sight of the breakfast tray on the table, still untouched. . . .

Robert Kennedy's aide John Seigenthaler soon found himself tearing down the highway from Birmingham to Montgomery with a White House telegram in his pocket. On this, the fifth day of what had begun as an ad hoc goodwill trip, he was pressed into higher service as an emissary of the President. He rushed directly to the Alabama capitol. Escorted into the governor's office, he confronted not only Patterson but the wary faces of all the Alabama cabinet members, convened around a long table for an extraordinary night session.

"Glad to see you. You're a Southerner," Patterson remarked on hearing Seigenthaler's Tennessee accent. He followed this hearty welcome with an angry oration, which Seigenthaler decided was largely for the benefit of the assembled Alabama politicians. "There's nobody in the whole country that's got the spine to stand up to the goddamned niggers except me," Patterson declared, using the word "nigger" with casual defiance. "And I'll tell you I've got more mail in the drawers of that desk over there congratulating me on the stand I've taken against what's going on in this country . . . against Martin Luther King and these rabble-rousers. I'll tell you I believe that I'm more popular in this country today than John Kennedy is for the stand I've taken." Sometime later, after more rhetoric and some earnest bargaining over the best way to get the Freedom Riders out of Alabama, he invited Seigenthaler to use his personal telephone, there in sight of the Alabama witnesses, to report the results to Robert Kennedy.

"He's given me this statement," Seigenthaler told Kennedy, looking at his notes: "'The State of Alabama has the will, the force, the men, and the equipment to give full protection to everyone in Alabama, on the highways and elsewhere.' He says he does not 'need or expect assistance from the federal government.'"

"Does he mean it?" Kennedy asked Seigenthaler.

"I think he does," Seigenthaler replied. Then he turned to Patterson. "Governor, he wants to know if you mean it."

"I've given my word as governor of Alabama," said Patterson, and he repeated his statement so loudly that Kennedy could hear it through the receiver in Seigenthaler's hand. . . .

Policemen herded the startled Freedom Riders onto the bus, and, as reporters dashed to their cars to follow, the St. Petersburg Express raced through downtown Birmingham, escorted by police cars with sirens wailing. The highway patrol picked them up at the city line, and the entire convoy—shadowed by FBI observers, plainclothes state detectives, and a highway patrol airplane, plus the trailing reporters—headed for Montgomery at speeds nearing ninety miles per hour. The Freedom Ride, paralyzed since the Mother's Day beatings, resumed at 8:30 A.M. on Saturday, May 20. In the interim, future congressman John Lewis and the other Nashville students had endured six days and nights on a roller coaster between joy and fear, exhilaration and boredom—largely uninterrupted by sleep—and several of them reacted to the moment of triumph by dozing off. Attorney General Kennedy, relieved at last, went out for a long horseback ride through the Virginia countryside. . . .

John Lewis, selected to speak for the group, stepped first off the parked bus and paused before a semicircle of reporters on the platform. As other reporters rushed up in front of him, and the Freedom Riders filled in behind, Lewis surveyed a terminal area that was familiar to him from scores of bus rides home to nearby Troy, where as a boy he had preached to the chickens. Now all the platforms and streets and parking lots were deserted. Aside from the drivers of a few taxis parked in the distance, the only people he could see beyond the reporters were a dozen or so white men hidden in a shadowy entrance to the terminal. Lewis felt an eerie foreboding. "It doesn't look right," he whispered to a companion.

Facing a battery of cameras, microphones, and notepads, Lewis got halfway through an answer to the first press question before falling strangely silent, transfixed by what he saw coming up behind the reporters. Norman Ritter, the Time-Life bureau chief from Atlanta, reacted to Lewis' face by turning to confront the dozen white men who had been standing in the door. He held out both arms to create a boundary for the interview, but the men, brandishing baseball bats, bottles, and lead pipes, pushed past him. One of them slapped Moe Levy of NBC News, and this first act triggered a seizing and smashing of cameras and equipment.

"Let's all stand together," said Lewis, as the Freedom Riders retreated backward along the enclosed loading platform. Hemmed against a railing that ran along a retaining wall, they stood helpless as the white men barreled into them. Some of Lewis' group jumped, some were pushed, and some were literally thrown over the railing onto the roofs of cars parked in the Post Office lot below. Those who did not take their luggage with them were soon pelted with their own suitcases. Above, on the platform, reporters who objected, or who tried to take photographs of the attack, were set upon by a small mob whose full fury was now released. The enraged whites smashed *Life* photographer Don Urbrock repeatedly in the face with his own camera. They clubbed Norman Ritter to the ground, beat a Birmingham television reporter, and chased the reporters who escaped.

Down below, the Freedom Riders realized that whites who had been secluded at various observation posts were closing in on them from all directions. Some stalked and some charged, egged on by a woman in a yellow dress who kept yelling "Get those niggers!" Fighting panic, the Freedom Riders made their way to two nearby Negro taxis and tried to send the seven females away to safety. Four of the five Negroes jumped into the backseat of the first taxi, whose driver had a little boy with him on the front seat. "Well, I can't carry but four!" cried the driver, when he saw that he was drawing the attention of the onsurging whites. There was no time to argue. The Freedom Riders shoved the fifth female Negro into the front seat anyway. "Well, I *sure* can't carry them!" shouted the driver, eyeing Susan Wilbur and Sue Harmann, the two white students. Doors slamming, he drove off as the two whites were pushed inside the other taxi. Before the second driver had a chance to say that it was illegal for him to transport whites, the mob yanked him and his keys outside to prevent the car from leaving, then dragged the two women from the back. Others chased the male Freedom Riders, some of whom were trying futilely to act on John Lewis' shouted directions about how to zigzag to Columbus Street and climb the long hill toward the refuge of Ralph Abernathy's First Baptist Church.

The first taxi, filled with screams and shouts, found one of the two exits from the parking lot choked off by a stream of angry whites. Swerving around, bombarded with conflicting advice, the driver found the other exit blocked by cars. This was too much for him. He told the Freedom Riders that he was going to abandon the taxi. While some of his passengers tried desperately to calm him, others looked back in horror at the loading platform. They, along with several Alabama reporters standing closer, saw a dozen men surround Jim Zwerg, the white Wisconsin exchange student at Fisk in Nashville. One of the men grabbed Zwerg's suitcase and smashed him in the face with it. Others slugged him to the ground, and when he was dazed beyond resistance, one man pinned Zwerg's head between his knees so that the others could take turns hitting him. . . . A small girl asked what the men were doing, and her father replied, "Well, they're really carrying on." The Freedom Riders in the nearby taxi turned away in sickened hysteria.

Upstairs at a window of the Federal Building, his renowned dour composure already dissolved, Washington's observer John Doar was describing the sudden disaster over the telephone to Burke Marshall. "Oh, there are fists, punching!" he cried. "A bunch of men led by a guy with a bleeding face are beating them. There are no cops. It's terrible! It's terrible! There's not a cop in sight. People are yelling, 'There those niggers are! Get 'em, get 'em!' It's awful." One of Robert Kennedy's secretaries was taking notes on an extension phone. Marshall, still listening to Doar, asked another one to track down the Attorney General. Less than five minutes after the bus door opened in Montgomery, official Washington knew that pipes and bare knuckles nullified all the painstaking federal-state agreements.

After political clashes between federal and state officials, National Guard soldiers escort a continuing Freedom Ride through Alabama into Mississippi.

— CHAPTER FOUR —

Freedom Rides II: MLK, the Kennedys, and National Politics, 1961

The Freedom Rides attracted national publicity as contending forces gathered from all sides. King and his colleague Ralph Abernathy flew in from Atlanta on Sunday, May 21, after Saturday's spectacular violence at the Montgomery bus station. They found a number of bandaged Freedom Riders holed up in Abernathy's former church on

Ripley Street, next to the Alabama state capitol. Fifteen hundred local Negroes joined them for a community meeting that turned into an ordeal over the fate of those inside, besieged by a mob of three thousand angry white people who overturned and burned cars, threw rocks through the church windows, and repeatedly battered at the doors to capture or kill the integrationists.

Tension escalated through the night. King called Attorney General Kennedy several times with desperate appeals for help. Kennedy, in turn, jockeyed with Alabama Governor John Patterson over who should shoulder the legal responsibility and political risk of protecting the trapped Negroes. Tempers snapped more than once, notably when King complained that Kennedy should not have withdrawn some federal officers armed with tear gas. "Now, Reverend, don't tell me that," Kennedy replied. "You know just as well as I do that if it hadn't been for the United States marshals, you'd be dead as Kelsey's nuts right now!"

Confrontation subsided only briefly the next day. Once again, the vanguard Nashville students expanded nonviolence in the face of danger. Their conflicted debates absorbed local groups into common purpose. What began in stalemate over whether an integrated bus could move, literally, swelled into a historical movement of cascading influence.

[From *Parting the Waters*, pp. 466–91]

O n Monday, May 22,] the Freedom Riders themselves were all secluded in the home of Montgomery pharmacist Richard Harris. King was there, too, along with CORE's James Farmer, and student leader Diane Nash. By nightfall, James Bevel and James Lawson arrived from Nashville. . . . In all, more than twenty people from the major strains of American nonviolent protest were gathered together under one roof in the city of the bus boycott, just across the street from the parsonage where King had lived for five years. What kept the Freedom Riders publicly muted for the better part of two days was not the arrest warrants or the mobs, nor even the leadership mechanics of a new coalition. Instead, the silence masked a renewed student campaign to have King join them in witness. . . .

Diane Nash, once Ella Baker had coached some of the awe out of her, asked King point-blank to go with them. He would set an example of leadership that might raise the standard of nonviolent commitment everywhere, she said. King replied that he agreed with her. He wanted to go but was not sure, he said. Daddy King and others on the SCLC board had pelted him with caution by then, and his aides, having talked with the lawyers in Atlanta, jumped in with the argument that King was still on probation from his 1960 traffic arrest in Georgia—the sentence that the judge had re-imposed on him just before the Kennedy-Nixon election. If arrested now on the Freedom Ride, King faced an additional six months in a Georgia prison, said SCLC's chief of staff, Rev. Wyatt Walker, and what would the movement gain by having King in jail on a traffic charge?

The students, following Nash, made light of this objection. "I'm on probation, and I'm going," said one. "Me, too," said another. King withered visibly under the pressure, as he had done the previous October when the Atlanta students implored him to join the Rich's sit-in. In a final, tortured retreat, he said, "I think I should choose the time and place of my Golgotha." Some of the students recoiled from this naked identification with Christ himself, rather than with Christian mortals. Both King and the students drew back from the unbearable tension of the personal revelation, and King, alone with Walker, said, "I am the one who has to answer for what I do, and I'm not going!"

Walker soon went back to the students, and when the issue welled up again, he cut them off. "Look," he said sharply, "if Dr. King decides he's not going, that's it. He don't have to have no reason." The fire in his eyes stifled all further dissent. So did his abrupt switch to the double negative of street jargon, which Walker used to signal straight talk—all Negro, no polish, no nonsense.

The students generally resented Walker's imperious manner, but they were divided on King. Among the young preachers, James Bevel supported King's decision on the grounds that he could carry the message of the Freedom Ride to tens of thousands around the country. He cautioned his fellow students against making badges of their commitment. Paul Brooks, who had been arrested outside Birmingham on the first bus of Nashville reinforcements, said he wished King had simply acknowledged his fear. "I would have respected him more," Brooks confided. John Lewis bridled at any overt criticism of King, but even he found himself defensively repeating Lawson's teaching that in nonviolence you do not badger people or force them beyond their commitment. He was looking gently but painfully back on King, patronizing the man he revered. . . .

In the end, only twelve Freedom Riders stepped forward, nearly all from Nashville. They chose their mentor in nonviolence, Rev. James Lawson, as group leader for the trip. Suddenly, behind the dozen Freedom Riders, came an equal number of National Guard soldiers in full battle dress, carrying bayoneted rifles, and behind them came their commander, General Graham. Addressing the Freedom Riders from the front of the bus, he seemed radically different from the stern antagonist who had marched into First Baptist Church. "This may be a hazardous journey," Graham said softly. "We have taken every precaution to protect you. And I sincerely wish you all a safe journey." As he stepped off the bus, several of the students thanked him emotionally for the whiff of reconciliation. Outside, just before the bus pulled out at 7:06 A.M., King reached up to an open window and shook the hand of student rider Paul Dietrich, to wish him good luck.

A squadron of motorcycle policemen helped the bus push its way through the congestion around the station. The policemen dropped off at the city limits to leave the bus in the midst of an extraordinary procession numbering some forty-two vehicles—mostly highway patrol cars, their sirens wailing, with several dozen more reporters bringing up the rear. Supplementing the main convoy were FBI spotter cars at strategic checkpoints, helicopter escorts, and U.S. Border Patrol airplanes in high-altitude reconnaissance—providing reports to Attorney General Kennedy's office via Byron White's staging area back in Montgomery. After the procession hurtled past the first scheduled stop, at Selma, the Guard commander on board revealed that all intermediate stops had been canceled. There would be no terminals, no snack bars, no rest rooms during the entire seven-hour trip to Jackson.

The caravan maintained speeds of nearly seventy miles per hour except for two brief delays. When fear and indigestion made a Freedom Rider violently ill, vigilant Guardsmen formed a tight circle around him while he vomited on the side of the highway. The second stop occurred at the border town of Scratch Hill, Alabama, where the crest of a hill brought into view a long line of Mississippi Guardsmen and state police units, poised to take over. The Mississippi escort was even longer than Alabama's. As the Scratch Hill transfer was being made, a distraught James Lawson jumped from the bus to hold an impromptu press conference with the milling reporters. He protested that the enormous military escort was contrary to the Freedom Riders' entire philosophy. It was unnecessary, he told the reporters, many of whom, terrified themselves by news tips of dynamite ambushes ahead in Mississippi, thought Lawson was out of his mind. "We would rather risk violence and be able to travel like ordinary passengers," Lawson added. ". . . We will accept the violence and the hate, absorb it without returning it."

By then it was late morning, and a second group of fourteen Freedom Riders had bought tickets for the 11:25 Greyhound out of Montgomery. Among them were two CORE students from New Orleans, Jerome Smith and Doris Castle, and Henry Thomas, a veteran of the Anniston bus-burning ten days earlier, who had returned for a second ride. Group leader Lucretia Collins, a Nashville student who had been with the ride since Birmingham, conducted nonviolence workshops en route.

News of this second busload came as a seismic shock to Robert Kennedy. All the cajoling and commandeering for the two-state armored caravan had been predicated on the assurance that they would have to pull it off only once. Instead, the fragile trust of the Alabama and Mississippi authorities was shattered again. Their motivation for cooperating with Kennedy, in what they regarded as a compromise of segregationist principle, was to end the crisis in a way that discouraged further bus riders. With new riders at the station even before the Alabama fleet returned to Montgomery, they felt betrayed, ridiculous. Kennedy himself, scrambling madly to keep the agreement patched together this one more time, was angry enough to issue his first formal statement. His aides in Washington told reporters that this second busload had "nothing to do with the Freedom Riders.". . .

The New York Times, which gave King and the civil rights movement generally sympathetic coverage, opposed the extension of the ride. "They are challenging not only long-held customs but passionately held feelings," the paper declared. "Non-violence that deliberately provokes violence is a logical contradiction." A news story that same day, headlined "Dr. King Refuses to End Bus Test," cast the issue in a most negative light. "Some liberal Southerners of both races joined moderates and others today in asserting that the Freedom Riders should be halted," it began, consigning the renewed campaign to the far fringes of public support. This was the last page-one story on the Freedom Rides to appear in the Times. A Gallup poll in June showed that 63 percent of all Americans disapproved of the Freedom Rides. . . .

Shortly after midnight on June 15—the day before their representatives were meeting with Attorney General Kennedy worlds away in Washington—guards herded forty-five of the male prisoners from their cells into closed truck trailers. The trucks lurched out of Jackson with the prisoners sealed in darkness. When finally they tumbled out blinking into the dawn light, they found themselves standing beneath an observation tower just inside the barbed-wire gate of an enormous compound, surrounded by guards with shotguns. The warden welcomed them to Parchman Penitentiary. "We have bad niggers here," he warned. "Niggers on death row that'll beat you up and cut you as soon as look at you." He ordered them to follow him in a line of march to a cement-block processing building. . . .

The prisoners were left waiting there for what seemed like an eternity before being marched to shower rooms, where they bathed under the gaze of shotguns. More than one of them felt stabbing rushes of identification with the prisoners of the Nazi concentration camps. Then they went on another naked march along cement corridors to the maximum-security wing, where, locked two to a cell, they endured another long wait before the guards brought their only prison clothes—a T-shirt and a pair of pea-green boxer shorts. Left alone at last, they shouted out their relief in complaints about the skimpy, ill-fitting garments. "What's all this hang-up about clothes?" James Bevel cried out above the noise. "Gandhi wrapped a rag around his balls and brought the whole British Empire to its knees!" . . .

The emotional wave of the Freedom Rides collided with the Kennedy registration plan. At a SNCC meeting exactly one week after their release from Parchman, student Freedom Riders were shocked to hear some of their colleagues propose that SNCC (pronounced "snick") adopt as its "top priority" the voter registration drive being discussed with Harry Belafonte. They were talking of a mammoth operation of some 200,000 student workers—a force a thousand times larger than the Freedom Riders. Passionate arguments erupted. Those just out of prison objected that there was nothing Gandhian about voter registration, which they saw as conventional, political, and very probably a tool of the Kennedy Administration for getting "direct action" demonstrators off the streets. Voter registration advocates replied that they were ready to undertake the drudgery of registration work, intimating that the Freedom Riders had been seduced by the allure of martyrdom. . . .

At Highlander, three days of rancorous debate produced nothing more than a deadlock among the state delegations within SNCC. Charles McDew announced dramatically that he was going to break the tie by casting the chairman's vote in favor of the voter registration plan. Several direct-action advocates stalked out in anger. Ella Baker, trying desperately to keep her prized students from surrendering to the leadership preoccupations that had so vexed her at the NAACP and the SCLC, proposed that SNCC operate for a time as two cooperating wings—direct action under Diane Nash and voter registration under Charles Jones. Her compromise won grudging acceptance from everyone except a few direct-action diehards. Bernard Lee left SNCC permanently, as did the former leader of the Atlanta sit-in movement, Lonnie King. By the end of the conference, a grim joke went around that SNCC should have two doors for its dingy office, so that the rivals would not cross each other's path. . . .

King contained these divergent strains within himself. Drawn to both the martyrs and the rulers, he was exposed during the Freedom Rides to extremes of scorn and admiration that were unprecedented even for him. His relations with the SNCC students suddenly became intimate but touchy and complex, as did those with Robert Kennedy. So sensitive was King's name in public debate that the white Southern Baptist Convention—which was trying to make peace with President Kennedy after its shrill warnings against putting a Catholic in the White House—forced its seminary to apologize publicly for allowing King to discuss religion on the Louisville campus. Within the church, this simple invitation was a racial and theological heresy, such that churches across the South rescinded their regular donations to the seminary. "Steps have been taken to help prevent the recurrence of this kind of error," announced Rev. J. R. White of the Southern Baptist Seminary's board of trustees. . . .

On August 13, as the exhausted [SNCC] students were accepting Ella Baker's compromise, King made a day trip to New York to preach in Riverside Church. East German shock troops were throwing down barbed wire as the first line of a Berlin Wall, sealing off West Berlin. Full attention of the superpowers made that Cold War drama eclipse all other freedom stories of the year.

Bob Moses, a pioneer of grassroots tenacity, and a witness for the Student Nonviolent Coordinating Committee (SNCC).

— CHAPTER FIVE —

Bob Moses, SNCC, and Mississippi, 1960–63

The sit-ins and Freedom Rides touched off protests in locations across the South. Some flared sporadically. Others took hold, as in Nashville or Albany, Georgia. A general exception was the entire state of Mississippi, where racial repression and intimidation were so strong that Negroes found it pointless even to attempt a picket line. In 1961, more than four hundred Freedom Riders wound up imprisoned at Mississippi's notorious Parchman Penitentiary, but no local Negroes stepped forward to join them. Medgar Evers, the NAACP's state secretary for Mississippi, bravely recruited members on the stated platform of equal citizenship, and a few student groups agitated on Negro campuses.

In dire extremity rose a notable exception, Bob Moses, on a new model of grassroots leadership. If King was developing into a young patriarch like the biblical Moses, embellished with classical oratory, Bob Moses became a counter-Moses. He spoke softly, raised questions rather than answers, and took cues from local sharecroppers. Wandering alone for the student group SNCC, Moses explored the ethics of shared sacrifice with a signature refrain, "Don't we need a lot of leaders?" By example, paradoxically, he grew into a legend within the student movement on par with King in the larger world.

[From *Pillar of Fire*, pp. 50–57, 68,
Parting the Waters, pp. 712–14]

Mississippi started at the bottom. [In 1962], when Bob Moses appealed for refuge at a statewide meeting of NAACP chapter presidents, he brought with him only two teenage recruits and a record of anguish. Moses was not from Mississippi, nor an NAACP member. He was a twenty-seven-year-old New Yorker with a Harvard master's degree in philosophy, who had become an object of wonder since venturing into the southwest timber region around McComb on a solo mission for the Student Nonviolent Coordinating Committee, a youth organization that had grown out of the sit-ins. For trying to escort would-be voters to register, he had been arrested more than once, pummeled by a courthouse mob, and beaten severely near a town square in open daylight by a cousin of the Amite County sheriff. Still bleeding, he walked into the courthouse to file criminal charges, then testified against the cousin, and, until the local prosecutor advised him to flee for his life before a jury brought in the customary verdict of acquittal, continued doggedly to behave as though he possessed the natural rights of a white person. This presumption shocked Mississippi people more than the blood and terror.

John Doar sought out Moses to learn of the violence in Amite County, just as he had introduced himself to Medgar Evers on a previous clandestine tour of Mississippi—traveling incognito in khakis and boots, knowing enough to be fearful himself even as a high-ranking official of the Justice Department. A Republican from Wisconsin, Doar had been asked to stay on in the Kennedy Justice Department partly because he had pioneered a go-out-and-poke-around-for-yourself approach to civil rights lawsuits, which made him unusual among deskbound Washington lawyers. With Moses, Doar visited Negro farmers who were afraid to come to registration meetings because of the intangible reality of rural life—ominous messages maids and sharecroppers were hearing—and several were particularly worried about signs of anger on the part of E. H. Hurst, a state representative of local influence, against Herbert Lee, an NAACP farmer who attended Moses' registration meetings. Doar promised to drive out to Lee's farm on his next trip, but he found waiting at his office the next day, September 25, 1961, a message from Moses that Hurst had just shot Lee to death in full public view outside the Liberty cotton gin.

In nearby McComb, while Moses pressed in vain for arrest in the Lee murder, his youthful admirers went to jail from a sit-in that quickly inspired a spontaneous march of more than one hundred high school students. Failing to dissuade them, Moses and other in-gathered SNCC leaders went along as protective support until McComb police plucked them from the line, ran some through gantlets of enraged citizens, and eventually crammed Moses and seventeen others—virtually the entire national leadership of SNCC—into the drunk tank of the Magnolia, Mississippi, jail. They obtained release more than a month later on appeal bonds financed by Harry Belafonte, and Moses soon asked the NAACP county leaders to sponsor a second foray anywhere apart from the skittering violence around McComb. "We had, to put it mildly, got our feet wet," he wrote. "We now knew something of what it took to run a voter registration campaign in Mississippi.". . . .

When King was compelled to retreat from Albany, Georgia, Bevel and Nash hitched rides with their infant daughter across Alabama back to their mentor Amzie Moore's house in the Mississippi Delta. Bob Moses was there, too, starting voter registration again based from Greenwood, using a new placebo organization called COFO—the Council of Federated Organizations—as a channel for small foundation grants. Like the Montgomery Improvement Association for the 1955–56 bus boycott, and several umbrella groups since, COFO allowed civil rights groups to cooperate through a kind of truce office, and the new name also buffered white opposition because it lacked the fiendish stigma of the NAACP. Temporarily, at least, pastors who had been afraid to open their doors to the NAACP might be talked into hosting a COFO workshop.

Bevel returned in time for one of COFO's earliest church gatherings on Monday, August 27, [1962,] at Williams Chapel Baptist in the tiny hamlet of Ruleville. Preaching from Matthew 16:3, he waved off individual fears of poor sharecroppers along with the presumed advantage of all-powerful Mississippi segregationists who, like the hypocrites denounced in his text, could not "discern the signs of the time." Just as the biblical hypocrites could read the stars in the heavens but not hearts, cried Bevel, the segregationists could run the space program but not see that freedom was sweeping the whole world. In America, freedom meant the vote, and in Sunflower County, where nearly three quarters of the potential voters were unregistered Negroes, the vote meant that meanness and hatred and suffering could be reduced if only the least of these would step into the Indianola courthouse to register.

Among those answering the call for raised hands was Fannie Lou Hamer, the twentieth child of sharecroppers. Short and stout at forty-one, she walked with a limp and was semiliterate in all subjects except biblical wisdom. Hamer had come to see whether this odd Mississippi preacher fit the reputation spreading on the plantations, and having caught Bevel's fire, she showed up that Friday among eighteen volunteers for what amounted to a mass registration attempt and a major word-of-mouth news story. There was no violence at the courthouse, but the Highway Patrol arrested Moses again on his way back to Ruleville. That night, the owner of the Marlow plantation evicted the Hamers from their shack of the past eighteen years, not so much on his own account, he told the Hamers—he could understand why somebody might want to vote—but for the gossip her action instantly stirred against him among the neighbors. Hamer presented herself as a refugee at a registration meeting, never to return home. The hostile climate stifled any sympathy local whites felt for her, and clerks at the welfare office declined even to accept her application for emergency surplus food until Diane Nash fired off a letter to Washington on her behalf, reminding the U.S. Secretary of Agriculture that treatment of Hamer violated the laws under which Sunflower County received nearly all its public relief funds. The new Delta project registered practically no new voters, but reprisals gained recruits one by one. . . .

In the fresh mayhem of the Greenwood COFO office, Moses spent hours discussing a trap within the circular powerlessness of racial subjugation itself: how to gain the vote without literacy, and literacy without the vote. One theoretical remedy was somehow to remove the literacy requirements in favor of universal suffrage, but such ideas touched the rawest nerve of the conflict between race and democracy. "We killed two-month-old Indian babies to take this country," one white voter explained succinctly to the press, "and now they want us to give it away to the niggers." On the literacy side of the trap, against generations of ignorance and segregated, dilapidated Negro schools, COFO workers grasped for small-scale relief from Martin Luther King's new Citizenship Education Program, which offered intensive, one-week adult literacy courses near Savannah and Charleston. James Bevel and Diane Nash petitioned King to open a third citizenship school in the Delta. Nash urgently lobbied for the schools at the Carnegie Hall fund-raiser, but King's administrator, Andrew Young, rejected the plan as unrealistic. "The chances are that you would be closed and the property confiscated in short order," he wrote, "that is, if it wasn't bombed first." Young's worry was hardly far-fetched; he had inherited his program after the Highlander Folk School suffered such a fate in Tennessee. He teased Nash in a postscript over her edgy, possessed mood, which was common among those who left and reentered Mississippi's reality warp. "Diane, you really should have stayed over a day or so in New York so we could have 'done the town,'" Young advised. "Then you'd have had to go back to Mississippi and work hard to get rid of your guilt.". . .

[By February 1963,] more than six thousand sharecroppers stood in line outside the Wesley Chapel in Greenwood, hoping for some of the emergency supplies gathered from Northern donors. A smattering of American Indians among the Negroes bore witness to the Delta's lingering Indian heritage. (LeFlore County and its principal town, Greenwood, were named for the last high chief of the Choctaw nation, Greenwood LeFlore.) Even after some thirty tons came in by plane and truck, there were enough cheese and blankets only for about a seventh of those in line, more than 90 percent of them illiterate. As the Negroes least likely to take or pass the registration test, these destitute sharecroppers seemed a poor choice of clientele to the COFO registration workers. But the registration campaign was moribund anyway, with only fifty Negroes having taken the test in the preceding eight months, and sharecroppers had begun to trickle into the nighttime registration meetings. By Delta standards it was a great event when seventy-five of them showed up on February 11 to hear James Bevel. He sang freedom songs, then preached on the connection between the voter registration effort and the cutoff of food. "Don't let the white man do your children as he has done you," he pleaded.

Outside the Justice Department, Attorney General Robert Kennedy faces one of many crowds outraged by police attacks on Negro children in Birmingham.

CHAPTER SIX

A National Firestorm from Birmingham, 1963

Converging events pushed Martin Luther King toward a fateful decision in 1962. Late that September, he convened the sixth annual convention of his Southern Christian Leadership Conference (SCLC) in the bastion city of Southern segregation, Birmingham, Alabama. A member of the American Nazi Party darted from the audience there to slug him repeatedly, and King, while recuperating, watched dramatic television news at the University of Mississippi.

He reflected glumly to close associates. More than eight years after the Supreme Court's clarion *Brown* decision, it was requiring thousands of U.S. soldiers to guarantee the admission of only one Negro student, James Meredith, at Ole Miss. The defenders of segregation were mobilizing, King observed, and the civil rights movement may be losing its window in history to secure lasting change. Moreover, he expressed frustration with his customary role as a "fireman" called in to revive local protest by others. Over the past nine months, he had gone to jail three times in Albany, Georgia, without encouraging results.

King resolved to design and mount a showdown campaign in Birmingham. Significantly, fearing internal opposition, he did not tell most of his own SCLC board members. Also significantly, wiretaps on his advisers alerted the FBI to secretive preparations beginning in January of 1963. Rev. James Lawson trained nonviolent volunteers, for instance, and Rev. Fred Shuttlesworth recruited local pastors in Birmingham.

Daily demonstrations stepped off on April 3, but the carefully phased plan fizzled in the face of arrest and intimidation by Birmingham's fearsome police commissioner, Bull Connor. Increasingly desperate measures gained no momentum. King himself submitted to eight days in an isolation cell, where he composed a letter destined to become a classic, but the outside world ignored his eloquent appeal along with the dwindling marches to jail.

By late April, with King's great gamble on the verge of surrender, Negro households began to hemorrhage over rumors that he might enlist marchers of high school age. This was the brainchild of James Bevel and his wife, Diane Nash, from the Nashville workshops. Parents called the notion cowardly and cruel—even insane—until Birmingham's D-Day shocked the world with steadfast youth legions down to six years old. *The New York Times* joined prominently in a firestorm of daily headlines: "Birmingham Jails 1,000 More Negroes."

[From *Pillar of Fire*, pp. 86–87;
Parting the Waters, pp. 802–25; *Pillar of Fire*, 108]

The blow landed with strange subliminal force. Nearly everyone reacted to the riveting images of dogs biting children, but public commentaries were loath to analyze the phenomenon, and retrospectives on the decisive political tactic were nowhere to be found. Insofar as public figures did comment specifically on children's jail marches, they were critical. . . . Still, beneath the silence and disparagement alike, there were signs of a rare, deeper tribute in the form of dumbstruck attachment. . . . Where reason had twaddled, a tide of emotion swept forward conviction that segregation was fragile and that human nature contained untapped reserves for improvement. From the first children's march on May 2, *The New York Times* published more stories about race in the next two weeks than during the previous year. Attention spilled from the news to the editorial and features pages, and from there to a rash of projects on racial subjects that within a year published new and reprinted books at the rate of nine per week. . . .

King was in Cleveland, Ohio. It was May 15—"some six or seven weeks," as he put it, since the birth of his daughter at the commencement of demonstrations in Alabama, and nearly two weeks since the first children's march of May 2. Only after he emerged from Birmingham's long dark tunnel did he begin to see how drastically everything, including his own life, had changed. Mobbed at the airport, King motorcaded like an astronaut through the streets of Cleveland to St. Paul's Episcopal Church for what amounted to the first white mass meeting of the civil rights movement. His separate constituencies suddenly blended into jumbled hordes. In a whirlwind twelve hours, he gave six speeches and a television interview. . . . The evening's live audience exceeded ten thousand, and the SCLC netted $15,000 from the offerings. "I've never seen a more aroused response," King exclaimed from one pulpit. . . .

Burt and Norma Lancaster hosted a reception in Beverly Hills, for which California governor Edmund G. Brown had sent out the invitations. A brassy Hollywood lawyer got down to business by announcing that it took $1,000 in hard cash to run the SCLC movement each day. Paul Newman wrote the first $1,000 check, singer Polly Bergen the second, actor Tony Franciosa the third. Actors John Forsythe and Lloyd Bridges contributed, as did the wife of basketball star Elgin Baylor. Marlon Brando mumbled a warning against "what-we-have-doneism" and bought a week of the movement for $5,000. Sammy Davis, Jr., matched the reception's total receipts with his own pledge of $20,000. Together with Wrigley Field contributions of $35,000, the evening brought the SCLC $75,000. Awed by the glitter and money, a *Jet* reporter wrote that "We Shall Overcome" rang out from the Lancaster home "like Wings Over Jordan in Beverly Hills."

Then King flew to a different kind of awe in the heartland: riding in an open car amid a fleet of limousines, rushing through the streets of Chicago behind the roar of police motorcycles and the wail of sirens to city hall for an official welcome by Mayor Richard Daley. The mayor, looking only slightly uncomfortable, joined the motorcade to the city-owned McCormick Place on the shore of Lake Michigan, where for nearly an hour he stood backstage with King as Mahalia Jackson fussed over them, straightening their ties and thundering at the stagehands and musicians who were delaying her big night. Then, finally, Mayor Daley welcomed the heroes of Birmingham. In his own speech King was hard-pressed to match the dueling headliners—Mahalia Jackson, queen of gospel, appearing for once with her archrival Dinah Washington, queen of the blues. The three of them held the overflow crowd until two o'clock in the morning, when young

Aretha Franklin topped them all with her closing hymn. Only twenty-one, already a battered wife and the mother of two children aged six and four . . . Franklin still remained four years away from crossover stardom as Lady Soul, but she . . . wrung them all inside out with the Thomas Dorsey classic "Precious Lord, Take My Hand," and by the time she finished few doubted that for one night they had held the most favored spot on earth. Franklin herself was so moved by the privilege of singing at King's rally that she slipped four $100 bills into Mahalia Jackson's hand on stage. . . .

Birmingham had suddenly changed King from a tireless drone on the speaking circuit to the star of a swarming hive. And beyond the rallies of support as far away as Birmingham, England, and Havana, Cuba, a host of spontaneous actions made news. Clergymen in the manicured white suburb of Greenwich, Connecticut, united to fight segregation. Duke University announced the admission of its first Negro students. Demonstrations spread arrests to a new city almost every day in May: 34 arrested in Raleigh, nearly 100 in Albany, 400 in Greensboro, 1,000 in Durham, North Carolina.

The same winds that lifted King from behind struck the Kennedy Administration in the face. Intelligence reports noted that the Soviet Union broadcast 1,420 anti-U.S. commentaries about the Birmingham crisis during the two weeks following the settlement—seven times more than at the worst of the Ole Miss crisis, nine times the peak during the Freedom Rides. When President Kennedy sent a message on May 21 to a summit conference of the independent African nations, stressing the importance of unity in the free world, Prime Minister Milton Obote of Uganda replied with an official protest against the firehoses and "snarling dogs" of Birmingham. President Kennedy saw that even one of his own soldiers was allowed to march in support of the Birmingham movement at a remote Air Force base in South Dakota, and that such a piddling event made the news. "How the hell did this happen?" he demanded of his aide for civil rights, Lee White.

On May 20 and 21, President Kennedy privately consulted his government on the repercussions from Birmingham. One problem, the Attorney General told the full cabinet, was that the federal government itself maintained a largely segregated work force. In Birmingham, "there weren't any

Negroes that held any positions where anybody could see them," and the businessmen had demanded to know, "'Why should we hire Negroes? *You* don't hire Negroes.'" Kennedy introduced Civil Service Commission chairman John Macy for a quick summary of the numbers elsewhere: of 405 U.S. Treasury employees in Nashville, there were four Negroes, all clerks; of 249 Agriculture Department employees in Nashville, two Negro clerks; of 114 employees at Labor and Commerce, no Negroes at all. Rolling out similar statistics for other Southern cities, Macy endorsed the Attorney General's view that it was better to address them early than "just wait until they flare up.". . .

By the end of the meeting, President Kennedy leaned toward proposing a civil rights bill. Nearly everything about it was in flux, however, and his own political people were far from reconciled to a public accommodations section. For the immediate future, Robert Kennedy was in a rush to hold a series of off-the-record meetings at the White House with governors, mayors, theater owners, chain-store owners, lawyers, preachers, civil rights leaders, and others—both to lobby for national action and to take soundings on their course. The President agreed, stipulating only that any meeting with Martin Luther King come late in the series. "Otherwise, it will look like he got me to do it," said the President. "The trouble with King is that everybody thinks he's our boy, anyway. So everything he does, everybody says we stuck him in there. We ought to have him well surrounded . . . King is so hot these days that it's like Marx coming to the White House. I'd like to have some Southern governors, or mayors, or businessmen first. And my program should have gone up to the Hill first.". . .

On May 30, King sent telegrams to President Kennedy and the Attorney General requesting a personal audience with them "to avert an unnecessary national calamity." What King hoped was that now, with the worldwide protest over Birmingham, he could finally persuade President Kennedy to issue the executive order against segregation. Stanley Levison, King's closest white friend and adviser, endorsed his strategy with the observation that no Administration had ever been so worried about the Negro problem as the Kennedys were now. FBI wiretaps on Stanley Levison's home phone enabled J. Edgar Hoover to dispatch his couriers with advance warning of King's telegrams—of King's expressed hope "to put so much pressure on the President that he will have to sign an Executive Order"—and to note that King was formulating such plans with a "secret member of the Communist Party." King, of course, did not know of the wiretap, nor of Kennedy's earlier resolve not to receive him while he was so "hot." All he knew was that Lee White declined his request on the grounds that President Kennedy was too busy.

It was almost midnight on June 1 when King placed a conference call to Levison and Clarence Jones to discuss his response. He opened with a bit of news for the New Yorkers, telling them that NAACP leader Roy Wilkins was in jail in Jackson, Mississippi. Medgar Evers had called again, he said, but had disclosed none of his plans because he believed the Jackson police were tapping his phone. For King, Wilkins' first arrest in nearly thirty years was a sober but hopeful development. "We've baptized brother Wilkins," he said. Levison said they could expect new things like that to spread through the Southern cities, and he suggested a special SCLC meeting to discuss how to respond. Jones talked of mobilization discussions he had attended with New York church groups.

King cut them off. "We are on a breakthrough," he said gravely. "We need a mass protest." They must take advantage of the fever he felt sweeping ahead of them. What he had in mind was a "mass march" on Washington "and also a unified demonstration all over America." . . . King told them to contact the venerated trade union leader Philip Randolph and signed off, leaving Jones and Levison to soar away in appreciation of his sudden audacity. For days they treasured this one phone call among thousands. In an uncharacteristic gush, Levison told Jones' wife, Ann, that "you tingled" when King talked that way about historical opportunity, and he confessed that his own ideas were "a step behind Martin." Jones kept saying he was "thrilled by the conversation." "We both know that Martin is a very cautious and thoughtful person," declared Jones, "and he is saying the hour is now." The FBI's wiretap stenographer summarized their glowing reprise: "They agree that all sorts of very exciting things are happening.". . .

[On Tuesday, June 11], as President Kennedy and the Attorney General anxiously awaited the outcome of the school segregation showdown with

Alabama Governor [George] Wallace, a telegram came in from Martin Luther King on the "beastly conduct of law enforcement officers at Danville." Asserting once again that "the Negro's endurance may be at the breaking point," King implored the Administration to seek a "just and moral" solution. . . . There was a rougher, public message from King on the front page of *The New York Times* . . . [which] quoted his plea that, above all, President Kennedy must begin speaking of race as a moral issue, in terms "we seldom if ever hear" from the White House.

Given his recent sensitivity to King's opinions, these urgings may have influenced President Kennedy's extraordinary decision to make what amounted to an extemporaneous civil rights address on national television. The causes were uncertain because the notion of a speech came so suddenly from the President himself, without a trace of the usual gestation within the government. When he startled his advisers on Tuesday with the thought that he might announce his civil rights legislation on television that night, no one liked the idea. . . . There was no speech draft. There had been no consultations with Congress or anyone else on what the President planned to say. To make a naked dash that very night on so sensitive an issue seemed like the worst sort of presidential whim, but Kennedy refused to let it go. . . . Toward six o'clock that evening, President Kennedy ordered fifteen minutes of network time at eight. He gave speechwriter Ted Sorensen some general ideas and some scraps he liked from Negro aide Louis Martin, then sent him off to write a speech within two hours.

Minutes before eight, Sorensen came into the Cabinet Room with a draft that President Kennedy found workable but stiff. He began tinkering to add paragraphs of fervor and rhetoric, dictating to Evelyn Lincoln while Sorensen cross-dictated to Gloria Liftman. They retyped pages and fragments, inserting them here or there in the stack as opinions changed in the mad fit of purpose. [Burke Marshall] was aghast with the realization that there would be no finished text—that the leader of the free world was about to ad-lib on national television—but as the seconds ticked away the President was at his best, wired both hot and cool. "Come on now, Burke," he prompted. "You must have some ideas."

The President's first peroration before the cameras was a bit awkward, on the refrain "it ought to be possible," but then he broke through with a sketch from Louis Martin contrasting the life chances of two newborn American babies, one white and one Negro. "We are confronted primarily with a moral issue," he declared. "It is as old as the Scriptures and is as clear as the American Constitution. The heart of the question is whether all Americans are to be afforded equal rights and equal opportunities, whether we are going to treat our fellow Americans as we want to be treated."

These words brushed along a religious course that was starkly out of character for the worldly President. Their flow transformed even his approach to the global struggle:

> We preach freedom around the world, and we mean it. And we cherish our freedom here at home. But are we to say to the world— and much more importantly, to each other—that this is the land of the free, except for Negroes, that we have no second-class citizens, except Negroes, that we have no class or caste system, no ghettos, no master race, except with respect to Negroes?
>
> Now the time has come for this nation to fulfill its promise. The events in Birmingham and elsewhere have so increased the cries for equality that no city or state or legislative body can prudently choose to ignore them. . . . We face, therefore, a moral crisis as a country and a people. . . . A great change is at hand, and our task, our obligation, is to make that revolution, that change, peaceful and constructive for all.

Kennedy wandered on and off his text, outlining his forthcoming legislation. He kept inserting parenthetical phrases signaling that race was no longer an issue of external charity or deflection: "We owe them, and we owe ourselves, a better country." When he ran out of text, he coasted unevenly to the end. By then, it didn't matter.

In Atlanta, King drafted an instant response, with errors characteristic of his own uncertain typing and spelling. "I have just listened to your speech to the nation," he wrote. "It was one of the most eloquent[,] profound and unequiv[oc]al pleas for Justice and the Freedom of all men ever made by any President. You spoke passionately to the moral issues involved in the integration struggle." An equally excited Stanley Levison called King that night to say that President Kennedy had done "what you have been asking him to do." To Levison, the historic speech underscored the importance of their decision to make Congress, not President Kennedy, the focus of the Washington demonstration.

In Jackson, all three Evers children, including toddler Van Dyke, tumbled in their parents' bed, arguing over which television program to watch. Their mother had allowed them to stay up past midnight to find out what their father thought of the President's wonderful speech, and they all rushed for the door when they heard his car. Medgar Evers was returning from a glum strategy session. All but nine of the seven hundred Jackson demonstrators were out of jail. Local white officials were claiming victory untainted by concession. Both the white and Negro press portrayed the Jackson movement as shrunken, listless, riddled by dissension. Privately, Evers had asked for permission to invite Martin Luther King to join forces, but his NAACP bosses ignored the heretical idea. Finally home, Evers stepped out of his Oldsmobile carrying a stack of NAACP sweatshirts stenciled "Jim Crow Must Go," which had made poor sales items in Mississippi's sweltering June. His own white dress shirt made a perfect target for the killer waiting in a fragrant stand of honeysuckle across the street. One loud crack sent a bullet from a .30-'06 deer rifle exploding through his back, out the front of his chest, and on through his living room window to spend itself against the kitchen refrigerator. True to their rigorous training in civil rights preparedness, the four people inside dived to the floor like soldiers in a foxhole, but when no more shots came, they all ran outside to find him lying face-down near the door. "Please, Daddy, please get up!" cried the children, and then everything fell away to blood-smeared, primal hysteria. The victim said nothing until neighbors and police hoisted the mess of him onto a mattress and into a station wagon. "Sit me up!" he ordered sharply, then, "Turn me loose!" These were the last words of Medgar Evers, who was pronounced dead an hour later.

The Evers murder came at the midpoint of a ten-week period after the

Birmingham settlement when statisticians counted 758 racial demonstrations and 14,733 arrests in 186 American cities. Two men demanding integration chained themselves to the gallery of the Ohio legislature. An Alabama mob stoned the home of a white preacher who suggested that Negroes be allowed to worship in his church. . . . Like Kennedy's speech, the murder of Medgar Evers changed the language of race in American mass culture overnight. The killing was called an assassination rather than a lynching, Evers a martyr rather than a random victim—recognized as such with a post-funeral cortege by train to Washington and a family audience of condolence at the White House.

March on Washington, August 28, 1963: a gathering host fills Constitution Avenue en route to the Lincoln Memorial rally.

— CHAPTER SEVEN —

The March on Washington, 1963

The Kennedy Administration submitted comprehensive civil rights legislation that would ban employment discrimination and outlaw segregation in most places of public accommodation—restaurants, hotels, theaters, libraries, retail stores. King came to Washington brimming with optimism for a June 22 strategy meeting with President Kennedy.

Much to his dismay, however, Kennedy officials refused to discuss their new political alliance until King agreed to purge his movement of alleged Communist influences, especially his closest white adviser and friend, Stanley Levison.

President Kennedy took King alone into the White House Rose Garden. "I assume you know you're under very close surveillance," he warned. His grave manner astonished King, who thought the President behaved as though the White House itself might be bugged. King tried to make light of the allegations, then asked to see proof. He said everyone associated with the Negro movement had been accused of Communist ties, including the Attorney General. The President replied that evidence on Levison was too secret to share, coming from the highest levels of national security. To a stand off, King vouched for Levison's character and patriotism against persistent but vague accusations from President Kennedy.

Afterward, a shell-shocked King debated whether Levison's head was a hard political trade or the precursor to a witch hunt. Levison decided for him, severing their ties unilaterally. King labored to regain balance for the August 28 March on Washington for Jobs and Freedom. The approaching rally excited a similar clash of racial apprehension and hope, faith and paranoia. King's oratory at the Lincoln Memorial would soar in a famous, defining synthesis.

[From *Parting the Waters*, pp. 872–83;
Pillar of Fire, pp. 132–33; *Parting the Waters*, p. 887]

Public expectations brimmed with apprehension. In Washington, authorities from all sectors guarded against the possibility that marauding Negroes might sack the capital like Moors or Visigoths reincarnate. The city banned liquor sales for the first time since Prohibition. President Kennedy and his military chiefs were poised with pre-drafted proclamations that would trigger suppression by 4,000 troops assembled in the suburbs, backed by 15,000 paratroopers on alert in North Carolina. Washington hospitals canceled elective surgery. Some storekeepers transferred merchandise to warehouses to safeguard against looting. Chief Judge John Lewis Smith, Jr., notified his fifteen colleagues to be prepared for all-night criminal hearings, and practically no baseball fans protested when the Washington Senators postponed two days' games until Thursday, when the march would be safely over. . . .

According to march historian Thomas Gentile, twenty-one charter trains pulled in that morning, and buses poured south through the Baltimore tunnel at the rate of one hundred per hour. A jaunty young Negro finished a week-long journey on skates, having rolled all the way from Chicago wearing a bright sash that read "Freedom." An eighty-two-year-old bicycled from Ohio, and a younger man pedaled in from South Dakota. Small high school bands improvised on corners of the Mall. Determined high spirits converged from all directions in a kind of giant New Orleans funeral—except that here there was hope of removing the cause of the underlying pain, and here the vast acreage between the Capitol and the Washington Monument muffled the excitement with the dignity of open space. Among the tens of thousands of in-pouring whites, plainspoken workers from the UAW and other unions mingled with students and over-earnest intellectuals. Few of them were completely at ease in a swelling sea of dark faces, but nearly all of them forgot their apprehensions. They were swept away by what in fact was the ordinary transport of countless mass meetings, while movement veterans absorbed revelatory homage from palpable symbols of white prestige—the television cameras, movie stars, and dearest edifices of American democracy. A chorus of news cameras clicked as James Garner pushed through the crowd hand in hand with Negro actress Diahann Carroll; they were among dozens who had arrived on the Hollywood "celebrity plane" organized by Harry Belafonte and Clarence Jones. Even those who had attended a hundred mass meetings never had witnessed anything like Marlon Brando on the giant stage, holding up for the world an actual cattle prod from Gadsden, Alabama, as an indictment of segregationist hatred.

At the Washington Monument staging area, a public address system came alive shortly after ten o'clock with the voice of Joan Baez, who entertained the early-bird crowd by singing "Oh Freedom," a spiritual that Odetta had made popular. Odetta herself came on next, singing "I'm On My Way," and her mountainous voice prompted Josh White to jump up beside her out of turn. White, whose career reached back into the 1920s and 1930s, when March coordinator Bayard Rustin had been one of his sidemen, asked Baez to join them during a number, and soon Peter, Paul and Mary stepped in among them. The trio took the lead on one of their new hits, Bob Dylan's "Blowin' in the Wind," and then Dylan himself stepped out among them. He had just written a ballad about the death of Medgar Evers. It was a rare moment for folk music, as the performers on the stage had gained celebrity status for themselves and celebrity for their overtly cross-racial tradition. To underscore their respect for the movement, they brought on the SNCC Freedom Singers from Albany. Baez had just persuaded one of them, Bernice Johnson, to give up the study of opera for what became a luminous career as a performer and student of music derived from Africa. . . . A potpourri of Americana filled the interludes between songs. The first Negro airline stewardess led cheers. Norman Thomas, the old patrician Socialist, looked tearfully over the huge crowd and said, "I'm glad I lived long enough to see this day.". . .

Mounted in the eagle's eye of the Washington Monument, a CBS television camera showed viewers a thick carpet of people on both sides of the half-mile reflecting pool and all around the base of the Lincoln Memorial. At noon, nearly two hours before the rally began, the police estimated the crowd at more than 200,000. From this official number, friendly observers argued plausibly that late arrivals and high density justified talk of 300,000, and the usual effusions ran it upward to 500,000. By whatever count, the numbers reduced observers to monosyllabic joy. Within the movement, the gathering sea of placards and faces produced the most brain-numbing sight since the first ghost fleet of empty buses chugged through Montgomery. . . .

Once the leaders pushed their way up the steps of the Lincoln Memorial, they confronted renewed brushfires over the latest draft of John Lewis' speech. Union president Walter Reuther (of the United Auto Workers) was furious, saying that while Lewis was right to prod the Kennedy Administration, he was foolish to belittle the civil rights bill. Burke Marshall rushed from the Justice Department in the sidecar of a police motorcycle, bearing a revised draft that blunted Lewis' criticisms of the government. Archbishop O'Boyle did not care so much about the Kennedy image, but he did consider the "scorched earth" language to be unacceptably violent in tone, and he refused to give the opening invocation unless changes were made. Bayard Rustin improvised with music to cover the chaotic dispute backstage, where rumors were flying and Ralph Abernathy kept running around telling everybody to be calm. Peacemakers shuttled between clumps of aggrieved speakers with compromise wordings. In the central huddle, Lewis and Roy Wilkins wound up shaking fingers angrily in each other's faces until Rustin jumped in to appoint an emergency truce committee of Randolph, King, Lewis, and the Rev. Eugene Carson Blake, a prominent white clergyman from the National Council of Churches. . . .

Very little of the new undertow touched Lewis himself. When his turn came to face the vast host, he stepped forward to a long rumble of applause in tribute to the students of the movement. He began nervously, and in places he inserted a hint of a British accent to cover a slow, Alabama farm tongue, but the crowd soon warmed up his cadence. Even those who had never heard of James Farmer or Alabany, Georgia's C. B. King could tell by the way he spoke their names that Lewis was personally acquainted with those being beaten and jailed. His authenticity stirred a crowd that was sleepy from a long afternoon's drone of self-conscious speeches. From him, talk of living "in constant fear of a police state" did not seem extreme, and his refrain, "What did the federal government *do*?" came as a bracing dose of realism. Prophetically, he did not use the word "Negro," and alone of the speakers talked of "black people" and "the black masses." Crowd response swept him through difficult rhetoric of scolding, cold-eyed idealism:

> *My friends, let us not forget that we are involved in a serious social revolution. By and large, American politics is dominated by politicians who build their careers on immoral compromises and ally themselves with open forms of political, economic, and social exploitation.*
>
> *There are exceptions, of course. We salute those. But what political leader can stand up and say, "My party is the party of principles"? For the party of Kennedy is also the party of [Mississippi's segregationist Senator James] Eastland. The party of [liberal Republican Senator Jacob] Javits is also the party of [conservative Senator Barry] Goldwater. Where is our party? Where is the political party that will make it unnecessary to march on Washington? Where is the political party that will make it unnecessary to march in the streets of Birmingham?"* . . .

Although the program was running nearly a half-hour *ahead* of schedule, by a miracle from Bayard Rustin, people ached to stretch limbs and escape sunstroke. They were ready to go home. When Randolph introduced King as "the moral leader of our nation," small waves of applause lapped forward for nearly a minute in tribute to the best-known leader among them as well as to the end of a joyous day. Then the crowd fell silent.

It was a formal speech, as demanded by the occasion and the nature of the audience. By then, ABC and NBC had cut away from afternoon soap operas to join the continuous live coverage by CBS. King . . . recited his text verbatim until a short run near the end: "We will not be satisfied until justice runs down like waters and righteousness like a mighty stream." The crowd responded to the pulsating emotion transmitted from the prophet Amos, and King could not bring himself to deliver the next line of his prepared text, which, by contrast, opened its lamest and most pretentious section ("And so today, let us go back to our communities as members of the international association for the advancement of creative dissatisfaction"). Instead, extemporaneously, he urged them to return to their struggles ("Go back to Mississippi. Go back to Alabama . . ."), to believe that change would come "somehow" and that they could not "wallow in the valley of despair."

There was no alternative but to preach. Knowing that he had wandered completely off his text, some of those behind him on the platform urged him on, and Mahalia Jackson piped up as though in church, "Tell 'em about the dream, Martin." Whether her words reached him is not known. Later, King said only that he forgot the rest of the speech and took up the first run of oratory that "came to me." After the word "despair," he temporized for an instant: "I say to you today, my friends, and so even though we face the difficulties of today and tomorrow, I still have a dream. It is a dream deeply rooted in the American dream . . ."

The "Dream" sequence took him from Amos to Isaiah, ending, "I have a dream that one day, every valley shall be exalted . . ." Then he spoke a few sentences from the prepared conclusion, but within seconds he was off again, reciting the first stanza of "My Country 'Tis of Thee," ending, " 'from every mountainside, let freedom ring.' " After an interlude of merely one sentence—"And if America is to be a great nation, this must become true"—he took it up again: "So let freedom ring." By then, Mahalia Jackson was happy, chanting "My Lord! My Lord!" As King tolled the freedom bells from New Hampshire to California and back across Mississippi, his solid, square frame shook and his stateliness barely contained the push to an end that was old to King but new to the world: "And when *this* happens . . . we will be able to speed up that day when *all* God's children, black men and white men, Jews and Gentiles, Protestants and Catholics, will be able to join hands and sing in the words of the old Negro spiritual, 'Free at last! Free at last! Thank God Almighty, we are free at last!' " With that King stepped suddenly aside, and the March tumbled swiftly to benediction.

The March on Washington earned the capital letters of a landmark event by the end of the afternoon. Beyond the record-breaking numbers—upward of a quarter million—and the stunning good order that turned all the riot troops and plasma reserves into stockpiles of paranoia, the march made history with dignified high spirits. News outlets gushed over scenes of harmony—"White legs and Negro legs dangle together in the reflecting pool"—and Roy Wilkins congratulated Negroes for passing what amounted to a character test: "I'm so proud of my people." Police recorded only four march-related arrests, all of white people: one Nazi, two violent hecklers, and a health insurance computer* who drove to work with a loaded shotgun. The outcome so embarrassed predictions that march organizer Bayard Rustin gained credit as a fresh wizard of social engineering, whose command of scheduling and portable toilets had worked a miracle on the races. Overnight, Rustin became if not a household name at least a quotable and respectable source for national journalism, his former defects as a vagabond ex-Communist homosexual henceforth overlooked or forgiven.

A sense of relief raised the goodwill of the march into heights of inspiration, as millions of television viewers, including President Kennedy, heard a complete King speech for the first and last time that day. The occasion introduced King's everyday pulpit rhetoric as a national hymn. Despair wrestled deep in his voice against belief in democratic justice, producing his distinctive orator's passion, but the passion itself went to the core of the American heritage. From his reassurance of a common political ideal, the address spilled over into fresh cultural optimism. Although King's peroration invited polyglot America—"*all* God's children, black men and white men, Jews and Gentiles, Protestants and Catholics"—to join in a spiritual song of African origin, most observers pictured integration in reverse as a journey made comfortable by the ability of Negroes to behave like white people. *Life's* review issue on the march, with Bayard Rustin on the cover and a text evoking "beatific calm," presented a signature couple marching in crisp matching overalls, captioned "Negro Gothic . . . reminiscent of famous Grant Wood painting.". . .

What quickly swept the press of both races was the "Dream" sequence, which stamped King's public identity. Critics would point out that the

---

* In 1963, a dozen years before the dawn of the microcomputer industry, the word "computer" popularly referred not to a machine but to a person who made computations.

dream was ethereal, and people who yearned for simple justice would object that the content was too simple. Still, precious few among millions detected lightness or naïveté in the speech. On the contrary, the emotional command of his oratory gave King authority to reinterpret the core intuition of democratic justice. More than his words, the timbre of his voice projected him across the racial divide and planted him as a new founding father. It was a fitting joke on the races that he achieved such statesmanship by setting aside his lofty text to let loose and jam, as he did regularly from two hundred podiums a year.

At Birmingham's 16th Street Baptist Church, the Sunday morning blast that killed four young girls left mangled cars and shattered windows nearby.

— CHAPTER EIGHT —

Birmingham Church Bombing, 1963

King's oratory helped shape the March on Washington in permanent history. Like the *Brown* decision of 1954, this watershed event grounded the cause of civil rights firmly in the American experiment itself. Also like the *Brown* decision, however, the March conveyed a naïve gloss on challenges ahead. The foundation for interracial democ-

racy remained novel and weak in mass culture, its identity untested
against primal fears.

Since the Montgomery bus boycott, civil rights veterans had
learned to anticipate harsh reprisals in the wake of any hopeful celebration. This time, less than three weeks after the March, a seismic
crime struck on Sunday morning in Birmingham. Here too the reaction was national, sobering, and grim, a precursor to the Kennedy
assassination in November. Only a keyhole into history could foresee
that these traumas would help secure landmarks of tempered freedom
by 1965.

[From *Pillar of Fire*, pp. 133–45;
Parting the Waters, pp. 888–901]

Early in September, CBS doubled nightly coverage to launch television's first half-hour newscast, featuring news-anchor Walter
Cronkite. Two years in the making, the plan aimed to build the
prestige of the Cronkite program toward the political conventions in the
1964 presidential election year. For the premiere, President Kennedy
granted Cronkite an exclusive interview that opened with the President's
concession that civil rights had cost him heavily in a number of states crucial to reelection, especially in the South*, and ended with a discussion of
what President Kennedy called "a very important struggle" against a Com-

---

* "We are trying to do something much more difficult than any other country has ever
done," President Kennedy told Cronkite, reacting to criticisms of the administration's policies
on race. "A good many people who have advised us so generously abroad have no comprehen-
sion of what a difficult task it is that faces the American people in the '60s."

munist-led insurgency in Vietnam, where forty-seven American soldiers had been killed. Reviewers called the Kennedy interview "leisurely." While some critics welcomed the extra time for thoughtful or amusing "soft" stories (and complimented in particular Cronkite's segment on Japanese singers trying to master the English diction of "With a Little Bit of Luck" in the Tokyo production of *My Fair Lady*), others doubted that CBS could fill a thirty-minute report every night.

NBC waited a week to match Cronkite* with an expanded version of the Huntley-Brinkley news. Meanwhile, against the novelty and star power of Cronkite's debut, NBC presented a three-hour special on the race issue, entitled *American Revolution '63*. The entire program aired without commercial interruption, as regular sponsors declined to be associated with controversy, and the network itself showed signs of reluctance. Producers allowed no mention of segregated churches, or church activity on either side, for instance, and, to avoid hazarding any structural concept, they adopted the odd contrivance of segments shown alphabetically by the names of cities. An opening on protests in Albany, Georgia, gave way to a flashback on pre–Civil War abolitionists in Amherst, Massachusetts.

In rare lapses from professional aloofness, NBC narrators revealed the tension of a great personal leap, like trembling knees at a wedding. "There comes a time, there even comes a moment, in the affairs of men when they sense that their lives are being altered forever," began correspondent Frank McGee. ". . . We are experiencing a revolution." McGee told viewers that he had first sensed it years earlier as a local news director during the Montgomery bus boycott†, and other voices cited the culminating impact of televised violence against children: "The outrage in Birmingham, the sparks from this fell on every state in the Union."

Among numerous segregationists filmed expressly for the special, Governor Ross Barnett of Mississippi argued that the national turmoil was a

---

* ABC, then the third major network, stayed with a fifteen-minute nightly news program until 1967.

† Montgomery "was not an evil city," McGee said, speaking over footage of the boycott. "We didn't realize Negroes demanding better treatment could no longer be treated as teenagers demanding to stay out after 9:30."

sinister illusion created by television itself. "You are witnessing one more chapter in what has been termed the television revolution," Barnett declared. On the NBC screen, he introduced a pregnant new ideology rooted in the assertion that the news media were driven by a secret racial agenda, saying that the past year's coverage "publicized and dramatized the race issue far beyond its relative importance," and that this deliberate media bias served as "a smoke screen to hide the biggest power grab in American history." Barnett concluded that "the real goal of the conspiracy is the concentration of all effective power in the central government in Washington.". . .

On September 9—the date on which President Kennedy appeared exclusively on NBC's "Huntley-Brinkley Report," inaugurating the network's jump from fifteen to thirty minutes of nightly news—three Birmingham schools finally opened under court order for limited integration, but [Governor George] Wallace sent National Guard troops in to bar the Negro students. By some oversight, Wallace neglected to surround one school in a parallel case in Huntsville, with the result that Alabama's first Negro elementary-school student, six-year-old Sonnie W. Hereford IV, attended a previously all-white school that day. . . . Governor Wallace denounced federal intervention. On Friday, September 13, he flew to Baltimore and declared his intention to run in the 1964 Maryland presidential primary.

That Sunday was the annual Youth Day at the Sixteenth Street Baptist Church. Mamie H. Grier, superintendent of the Sunday school, stopped in at the basement ladies' room to find four young girls who had left Bible classes early and were talking excitedly about the beginning of the school year. All four were dressed in white from head to toe, as this was their day to run the main service for the adults at eleven o'clock. Grier urged them to hurry along and then went upstairs to sit in on her own women's Sunday-school class. They were engaged in a lively debate on the lesson topic, "The Love That Forgives," when a loud earthquake shook the entire church and showered the classroom with plaster and debris. Grier's first thought was that it was like a ticker-tape parade. Maxine McNair, a schoolteacher sitting next to her, reflexively went stiff and was the only one to speak. "Oh, my goodness!" she said. She escaped with Grier, but the stairs down to the basement were blocked and the large stone staircase on the outside literally had vanished. They stumbled through the church to the front door and then made their way around outside through the gathering noise of moans and sirens. A hysterical church member shouted to Grier that her husband had already gone to the hospital in the first ambulance. McNair searched desperately for her only child until finally she came upon a sobbing old man and screamed, "Daddy, I can't find Denise!" The grandfather helplessly replied, "She's dead, baby. I've got one of her shoes." He held a girl's white dress shoe, and the look on his daughter's face made him scream out, "I'd like to blow the whole town up!"

By then, ten-year-old Sarah Collins had staggered out through the gaping hole in the wall where the stone staircase had been. She was partially blinded, bleeding through the nose and ears from concussion. Her brother ran around screaming that his sister was dead, and in the addled shock it was some time before anyone understood he did not mean Sarah but older sister Addie Mae, fourteen. Ambulance medics scooped up Sarah Collins among some twenty others and headed for University Hospital. It registered dimly on Mamie Grier that Denise McNair and Addie Mae Collins were two of the four girls she had seen in the ladies' room minutes earlier. Grier took a chance that her car would start even though its windows were shattered, fenders curled, and part of a door blown off. She drove unsteadily away until stopped at one of the police roadblocks being thrown up around the city. Officers recruited a white man off the street to drive her car to the hospital, where she found her husband among the less seriously wounded. The hospital was a noisy blur of shrieks, hymns, television cameras, and shouted orders from crowd-control guards. Comforting stories circulated about how the pastor's injured daughter, four-year-old Susan Cross, had smiled so bravely when they wheeled her through a nearby corridor. Grier could say little more than "Those poor girls," a phrase she would repeat vacantly under sedation for the next two weeks. . . .

Secondary effects of the church bombing churned madly through the white population of Birmingham. A preacher cut short a segregationist rally at a Go Kart track. Heading home from the rally, a pair of Eagle Scouts fired their new pistol at two Negro boys riding double on a bicycle, killing a thirteen-year-old perched on the handlebars; the Eagle Scouts told police they had no idea what made them shoot. By late afternoon, the polite re-morse that had prevailed among policemen at the bomb site had hardened against real and anticipated reprisals from angry Negroes in the streets. Governor Wallace sent in three hundred state troopers. Typically, when officers came upon rock battles between young whites and Negroes, the Negroes ran while the whites welcomed the relief. Officers killed one flee-ing Negro by shooting him in the back of the head. Among civilian whites in general, reactions wound more softly in the same coil: a stab of sympa-thy and generalized remorse, followed quickly by resentment of exagger-ated accusations and then a growing sense of innocence. White attorney Charles Morgan passionately declared that he and all other whites shared guilt for the bombing because they had tolerated or encouraged racial hatred. "We all did it," he said. For this he became a pariah among whites, and his speech itself fed a tide of aggrieved self-vindication. "All of us are victims," insisted Mayor Albert Boutwell. . . .

Diane Nash and James Bevel heard the news in Williamston, North Carolina. . . . To answer the Birmingham crime with deeds of equal mag-nitude, their first impulse was to become vigilantes—to identify, stalk, and kill the bombers in the place of corrupted white justice. Bevel believed it could be done; he knew that the identities of lynchers tended to become more or less an open secret. In wild caroms of mood, Nash and Bevel swung from a "Black Muslim" option to a grand alternative as pioneers in nonviolence: to combine voter registration work in Mississippi with the tactics of Birmingham direct action, including the children's marches. They would raise a nonviolent army across the entire state of Alabama to converge upon Montgomery and settle for nothing less than the enfran-chisement of every adult Negro in Alabama. By Monday night they were possessed to propose the latter plan to movement leaders gathering for the funerals. Leaving their one-year-old daughter behind with Bevel, who stayed to tend a local movement, Nash set off alone by bus.

She reached Birmingham on Tuesday afternoon in time to hear Fred Shuttlesworth preach the funeral of Carole Robertson, after which Nash pushed her way through cordons of mourners and preachers' helpers to outline the concept for him. For a second time—as with her declaration that the Freedom Rides must be renewed—Nash put Shuttlesworth in the rare state of being ambushed by a posture more audacious than his. With Ralph Abernathy, Shuttlesworth already had advocated a bold march to Montgomery to place a funeral wreath at the Alabama statehouse, but Nash's proposal swept far past symbolic gestures. When Shuttlesworth asked her to reduce the plan to writing for presentation to Martin Luther King, Nash found a typewriter and wrote late into the night, setting down guidelines of military zeal and organization: ". . . Marching and drills in command and coordination of battle groups. . . . Instruction in jail know-how; cooperation or non-cooperation with jail procedures and trial. . . . Group morale while imprisoned. . . . Drill in dealing with fire hoses, dogs, tear gas, cattle prods, police brutality, etc. . . . Practice in blocking runways, train tracks, etc. . . ." She proposed to begin with Birmingham students straight from the funerals, fanning out across Alabama for recruitment and training toward the goal of laying siege to Governor Wallace's state government—"severing communication from state capitol bldg. and from city of Montgomery" with lay-ins, call-ins, park-ins, and a sea of nonviolent bodies. "This is an army," Nash concluded. "Develop a flag and an insignia or pin or button."

Carrying her finished proposal, Nash heard King preach the next day over the open caskets of the three remaining victims. "There is an amazing democracy about death," said King, who urged mourners to take from hard reality—"as hard as crucible steel"—a comfort in the message left behind. "History has proven over and over again that unmerited suffering is redemptive," he said. "The innocent blood of these little girls may well serve as the redemptive force that will bring new light to this dark city. . . . We must not lose faith in our white brothers. Somehow we must believe that the most misguided among them can learn to respect the dignity and worth of all human personality.". . .

That night, Diane Nash presented to King the germ of what became his Selma voting rights campaign in 1965. She was angry. . . . [She] pushed her way into King's room at the Gaston Motel, where a wake competed with phone threats and rumors of a visit to the White House. She seized time to distribute her plan for laying nonviolent siege against Montgomery, which

King received politely at best. Some waved off the proposal as inflammatory and apocalyptic—not to mention an abrupt shift out of Birmingham. Nash insisted that the first duty of movement leaders was to offer a constructive outlet for people burning with nonviolent spirit. When she lost the general attention of the room, Nash began to advocate the plan one-on-one, distributing copies, accusing the preachers of being too eager to rush off to Washington. The young Negro staff lawyer for the Justice Department, Thelton Henderson, would forward a copy by mail to Washington officials, who received it like a hand grenade. Burke Marshall called the document's attitude "revolutionary.". . .

By the time King reached Washington the next afternoon . . . Robert Kennedy announced that he saw no legal basis for sending marshals or troops to Birmingham. And just before five o'clock that afternoon, White House Press Secretary Pierre Salinger announced that President Kennedy had appointed two personal emissaries to mediate the racial crisis in Birmingham: former Army Secretary Kenneth Royall and former West Point football coach Earl Blaik. The Administration publicly set its response to the Birmingham bombing only minutes before the King group arrived at the White House. . . .

King, while not privy to the internal dynamics of the White House meeting, saw the public result on the front page of the *Times*: "Kennedy Says Birmingham Can Solve Its Own Problems." Such news fed the anxieties gnawing at him later in Richmond, where the SCLC assembled for its seventh annual convention. The giant four-day affair drew five hundred delegates for what was meant to be a celebration of the movement's breakthrough. Rosa Parks gave a short speech. . . . The Birmingham movement choir gave nightly concerts of freedom songs. A panel discussion on "The Power of Nonviolence" featured organizers now acquiring an aura of legend—Bayard Rustin, James Bevel, James Lawson, and C. T. Vivian. The convention heard reports from Gadsden, Danville, and ten other cities in the grip of showdowns inspired by Birmingham. Celebrity speakers included Dick Gregory, Roy Wilkins, Adam Clayton Powell, and two U.S. senators.

They all crowded into Richmond's Hotel John Marshall, a proud old facility that bent to its first integrated convention with strained civility. For the delegates, a different strain of dissension rippled in all directions on the supercharged emotions of the church bombing, making it difficult to maintain even the façade of movement idealism. . . . Wyatt Walker demanded nearly a threefold salary increase based on the SCLC's stupendous growth, while diverse critics charged that King's paralysis had put the SCLC out of business. King's "I Have a Dream" fame caused Ralph Abernathy's long-simmering jealousy to spill over into indignant complaints that his hotel room was not appointed as finely as King's, and finally into an inebriated elevator scuffle with a white man who did not share his low opinion of the room service. . . .

On September 27, King closed the convention with an address of abject confession. "I have kept silence," he admitted. ". . . In doing so, I have acted contrary to the wishes and the frustrations of those who have marched with me in the dangerous campaigns for freedom . . . I did this because I was naïve enough to believe that the proof of good faith would emerge. It is now obvious to me that this was a mistake." He talked of the unsolved bombings, the evasions of the Administration, and the elusive goodwill of the March on Washington. He accused the Administration of wanting to believe that a quiet march meant the revolution was over. "They could have made no bigger mistake," he said. ". . . We are more determined than ever before that nonviolence is the way. Let them bring on their bombs. Let them sabotage us with the evil of cooperation with segregation. We intend to be free." In conclusion, King . . . preached from his blend of sources: Jesus on loving one's enemies, Reinhold Niebuhr on justice, Abraham Lincoln on the ideal of common citizenship. King quoted Lincoln's reply to a vengeance-starved Unionist who resented his stubborn refusal to call the Confederates enemies: "Do I not destroy my enemies when I make them my friends?" He wobbled on a sensitive spot, desperate to move but stuck in melancholy, confessing that his leadership was "standing still, doing nothing, going nowhere."

SNCC leader James Forman (*3rd from left, holding pipe*) conducts a workshop in non-violent discipline. College volunteer Andrew Goodman (*in dark T-shirt*) would be murdered days later by a segregationist posse.

— CHAPTER NINE —

Freedom Summer, 1964

The movement, having seized national attention in 1963, hung in the political balance through national trauma after President Kennedy's assassination. President Lyndon Johnson suspended all other legislative business through the spring of 1964 in a determined effort to break the longest Senate filibuster in U.S. history, which blocked passage of the comprehensive ban on segregation in public accommodations. Clergy and seminary students mounted a round-the-clock prayer vigil for the bill on the Washington Mall. To underscore the continuing need, King led peaceful marches that endured white mobs and segregated jails in the nation's oldest city, St. Augustine, Florida.

In Mississippi, meanwhile, students and intrepid sharecroppers adopted desperate measures to break out of battered paralysis. Violent repression for years had blocked SNCC projects to register Negro voters even in small numbers, but many misgivings plagued a proposal to recruit some five hundred volunteers for the summer of 1964, mostly white students from elite universities. Some objected that such visitors would overshadow grassroots leaders. Others raised moral qualms about the calculated use of sacrificial lambs to compel notice from an otherwise indifferent world—asking whether a movement for racial justice should put privileged volunteers deliberately in harm's way.

Bob Moses withheld his own judgment for weeks, customarily fostering consensus through unfettered debate. Only after the death of his follower Louis Allen, yet another local Negro murdered without recourse, did Moses snap in February. "We can't protect our own people," he told the movement council as he threw his influence behind a Mississippi summer project to begin in June. A recruiting tour for student volunteers took Moses that April to Stanford University, where King had exhorted a far larger crowd the night before.

[From *Pillar of Fire*, pp. 295–96, 361–74]

Those stirred by the classical oratory of . . . King witnessed the stark contrast of Moses speaking in quiet soliloquy, following his own thoughts with what one listener recorded as "the rhythms of man crossing a stream, hopping from rock to rock." Reviewing the four years since SNCC students first went to Mississippi, Moses paid tribute to the unexpected teaching of sharecroppers. "If we have any anchor at all," he said, ". . . if there's any reason why we can skip around from the bottom of Mississippi to the top of the skyscrapers in Manhattan and still maintain some kind of internal sense of balance, I think a lot of it has to do with those people, and the fact that they have their own sense of balance." The farmers gave Moses a sense "that you had hit rock bottom, that you had some base that you could work with and that you could build on." For a long time it had been impossible to communicate the promise or terror of Mississippi because those outside "really didn't know and didn't have any way of understanding," he went on, but with the cumulative pounding of distant news, "and finally after Birmingham, the country came alive." A vocabulary was emerging for national questions "much deeper than civil rights," said Moses—automation, schools, the nature of cities—questions that affect "our whole international affairs" and "go to the very root of our society. . . . It just happens that the civil rights question is at the spearhead of all of these." No one recognized the signs because they fell upon Negroes, he said, "but when the Negroes take to acts of terror, they will know about it. The country will know about it." Preconditions of breakdown "exist already," he said. "They exist within the cities. . . ."

"Seventy percent of the Negro youth in Philadelphia are unemployed," he said. "It's a fantastic figure. It affects white people when they organize gangs and start hitting and shooting and fighting each other, and then maybe turn their violence into the street and attack property, which probably belongs to white people." Because Negro literacy had always been a political threat to the white South—"if you teach people who want to read and write, then they're going to want to begin to govern themselves"—heavy migration from Southern plantations—"every year there are 10 percent fewer jobs"—had delivered up two generations of refugees who were largely useless to the modern world. Their claim on the future clashed with the New York World's Fair's dazzling model of slumless cities for the year 2000, with plant-filled glass buildings connected by whizzing elevated sidewalks encased in tubes. "The deep irony of that really hasn't reached out across the country," said Moses. "All everyone was concerned with was, 'Don't mess up our World's Fair.' Whose World's Fair?"

Moses drew his Stanford audience into some of SNCC's internal arguments. "There are deep moral problems that are connected already with the summer project," he said, and mentioned Herbert Lee, "who was killed that summer [in 1961], was killed just as surely because we went in there to organize as rain comes from the clouds. If we hadn't gone in there, he wouldn't have been killed." Moses confessed that nonviolence could not insulate its believers from blood responsibility, nor answer "whether those people who are enslaved, in order to get their freedom, have to become executioners and participate in acts of terror and death, in what sense they do participate in it." He was posing those questions now to an auditorium full of recruits—potential replacements for Lee. "We're back in that same kind of dilemma," he said, his voice trailing off, "which can be put maybe not very precisely in terms of victims and executioners, and maybe not very philosophically, but still, when you come to deal with it personally, it rests very heavy." Several seconds later, realizing that the speaker had lapsed into silence, some four hundred students rose for a standing ovation that lasted several minutes. . . .

At the COFO center in Meridian, Mississippi, Louise Hermey of Drew University followed the first rule of her communications training on her first day as a summer volunteer: she called the Jackson COFO headquarters to report that an expedition had failed to return by the appointed check-in time of four o'clock Sunday afternoon [June 21, 1964]. Advised to wait an hour in case of unexpected delay, she called back at five and was told to activate the search procedure. . . . Fellow volunteer Edna Perkins, a nineteen-year-old student at Bryn Mawr College, sat down near Hermey's phone desk to write her first letter home, trying to explain why "we're all sitting here in the office being quietly nervous as hell": "This morning Mickey

[Schwerner], who's the project director, and [James] Chaney, a local staff member, and Andy [Goodman], who's a volunteer, all went out to one of the rougher rural counties to see about a church that was burned down a few days ago. . . . Still no word from the missing people," wrote Perkins. "It must be 11 by now. . . . Nothing to do but play ping pong or read and wait for the phone to ring. I've been reading *All Quiet on the Western Front.* . . ."

In Atlanta, Mary King "felt a prickly sensation," knowing that most of the movement people experienced enough to understand a delay of seven hours were still in Ohio for the training sessions. She called the Mississippi jails, posing as a reporter from the *Atlanta Constitution.* . . . With a cringe, she awakened the parents of volunteer Andrew Goodman in New York and notified Mickey Schwerner's wife in Ohio. Only yesterday, when Rita Schwerner stayed behind there to help with the second week's training, her husband, Mickey, had made the long drive to Meridian in a station wagon with James Chaney and six volunteers, including Louise Hermey, Edna Perkins, and Goodman. . . .

At Peabody Hall in Ohio, on the campus of the Western College for Women, Bob Moses greeted three hundred new volunteers on Monday morning with a meditative speech. "We've had discussions all winter about race hatred," he said. "There is an analogy to *The Plague*, by Camus. The country isn't willing yet to admit it has the plague, but it pervades the whole society." Staff people soon interrupted to huddle with him, after which Moses stared for some time at his feet. "Yesterday morning, three of our people left Meridian, Mississippi to investigate a church bombing in Neshoba County," he announced. "They haven't come back, and we haven't had any word from them."

Rita Schwerner appeared on the stage to organize a telegram campaign to members of Congress. She erased a map of Mississippi from the blackboard to write in large letters the names of her young husband and the two other missing workers. The fresh trainees could tell something was terribly amiss beneath the veneer of exaggerated composure. "It suddenly became clear that she, Moses, and others on the staff had been up all the night before," wrote one volunteer. During the scramble to write telegrams, Moses slipped out of the auditorium to sit alone on a small porch outside the college cafeteria. What had prompted his disclosure to the trainees was a report from Jackson that the jailer in Neshoba County now acknowledged having the three missing workers in cells there until sometime the previous evening. Moses drifted into solitary apprehension, not wanting to disclose his interpretation to Rita Schwerner. He sat on the porch for nearly six hours. Those who knew him best approached tentatively with hugs of consolation. "You are not responsible for this," Victoria Gray whispered. . . .

Claude Sitton's front-page story—"3 in Rights Drive Reported Missing"—appeared in the *Times* on Tuesday, June 23. . . . FBI Director Hoover insisted that he speak with the President at 4:05 P.M., six minutes after Johnson's call to Mississippi's Senator James Eastland. "I wanted you to know that we have found the car," he announced, adding that "we can't tell whether anybody's in there in view of the intense heat." Hoover regretted his dramatic, precautionary hedge about the bodies as soon as the President questioned him intently about why agents could not get close enough to look in the windows for telltale signs of burned bones or belt buckles. "You mean the car is still burning?" asked Johnson. In five more phone calls over the next four hours, Hoover introduced new exaggerations—"the entire inside of the car is melted into molten metal"—behind an adjusted, "offhand presumption" that the car was empty.

Senator Eastland called back in the midst of these updates to report that [Mississippi] Governor Paul Johnson wanted the President to send an impartial observer to examine evidence of civil rights fraud. Mississippi investigators had established that the COFO people had reported the three boys missing *in advance*, said Eastland, and the governor "expects 'em to turn up . . . claiming that somebody has whipped 'em, when he doesn't believe a word of it."

Johnson cagily heard him out. "Okay, now here's the problem, Jim," he said. "Hoover just called me one minute ago. . . ." Senator Eastland groaned to hear of the burned car, but quickly recovered his aplomb. "The governor says if you'll send some impartial man down here," he replied, "you'll get the surprise of your life. . . . There's no violence, no friction of any kind." . . .

Well into Tuesday night, Johnson conferred at the White House with Robert Kennedy and Burke Marshall on how, assuming the worst, to keep this likely triple murder from going unsolved, like the Birmingham church bombing, or from multiplying into similar crimes over the summer. Seeing little hope for initiative by Mississippi authorities, they discussed how to maneuver the FBI into the only state where Director Hoover steadfastly refused to open a full-fledged FBI office. . . .

President Johnson summarized the problem as a delicate manipulation of three distinct sovereignties: Mississippi, the United States, and his old friend J. Edgar Hoover. Perceiving a need for flattery with a sting, he fixed upon the opening for an "impartial observer," reasoning that Governor Johnson could not now withdraw his invitation, and he proposed to send the retired CIA director Allen Dulles. The idea at first seemed silly to the Justice Department officials, but Johnson explained how much Hoover hated Dulles, having wanted to be CIA director himself, and told tales about Hoover's sputtering mortification that Dulles already sat on the Warren Commission, positioned to protect the CIA at the expense of his beloved FBI. Dulles was the perfect motivational tool for the mission, reasoned the President. . . . The departing Justice Department officials, while variously uncomfortable with Johnson by background and taste, could not help marveling upon their first exposure to his style—an adroit, relentlessly unabashed application of raw personal chemistry to politics. . . .

In Ohio, Bayard Rustin met with long silences as he dissected the psychology of nonviolence for the second-week volunteers. They may not be able to say so, he argued, but their whole purpose in Mississippi was to love their enemies in the special sense of bearing witness to a redeeming, common nature with the most bestial Klansman and with Senator Eastland, the most callous defender of segregation—"to take power from those who misuse it, at which point they can become human, too." Many of the trainees watched the national news after Rustin's lecture. "Then it happened . . . ," one wrote home of a special report on CBS television. ". . . Walter Cronkite told how the whole country was watching Mississippi." James Forman and other familiar speakers from the Ohio training sessions appeared on the screen along with Senator Eastland himself, who declared that Negroes were perfectly free to vote. News film showed U.S. sailors, mindful of swamp snakes, poking through Bogue Chitto for the three missing workers on orders of President Johnson, and when the audio portion took up the movement anthem "We Shall Overcome," the volunteers in Ohio joined hands to sing along with the broadcast. "Stunned, I walked out alone into the night," wrote the correspondent. "Life was beautiful. It was perfect. These people were me, and I was them."

Against the void of the disappearance, the most ordinary news from Mississippi seemed charged to the trainees in Ohio. Detailed reports filtered north of baths in backyard tubs using water heated over a fire, of heart-stopping trips to mail letters in town under the heavy gaze of white eyes, and of vivid sensory overload where "you feel the heat, breathe the dust, smell the outhouses, hear the kids and the chickens.". . .

In Washington, with President Johnson and Justice Department officials looking on hopefully, Allen Dulles called J. Edgar Hoover at midday [Friday] from the Oval Office. Following the carefully prepared script, he reported that all the leaders of Mississippi had spoken highly to him of the FBI. For Hoover's sake, Dulles promised to use his family influence with the National Council of Churches to curtail funding for the incendiary summer project, and he sympathized with Hoover's complaint that the volunteers were irritating Mississippi white people, first by living in colored homes and second by indoctrinating colored people to vote. Then Dulles outlined his recommendation to the President that Hoover "ought to review the number of agents" in Mississippi. "I realize it's difficult for you," he said, but state officials would not enforce the law without "somebody looking over their shoulder a bit, and I think you're the only fellow that can do it."

Hoover gave ground, but suggested that U.S. marshals would be better than FBI agents for the "superhuman task." When he praised the marshals as "symbols of authority," who could deter civil rights violations, Dulles realized that his influence had crested. Motioning for help, he fended off Hoover with hasty excuses—"I'm in the President's office now, and I think he wants this office"—and gave up the telephone.

"Edgar?" said President Johnson. ". . . What he is sayin' there in substance is we want to . . . avoid the marshal thing and the troops thing. . . . I'd rather you send another fifteen people or twenty people." . . . Only the Bureau was respected enough to frustrate integrationist schemes for military occupation, he said, and cajoled Hoover until the Director agreed with the Dulles recommendations. "You get your men in there now," urged the President in a rush. He said the White House would announce that "we've asked for additional men, and you're gonna send 'em."

"Yes, that's right," Hoover replied. . . .

Bob Moses dampened optimism that whipped through the . . . second-week volunteers before they embarked for Mississippi . . . wondering if the volunteers had read any of the *Ring* novels by J. R. R. Tolkien on the weariness of constant attention to good and evil. His grim experience with segregationist violence ran ahead of the facts yet confirmed. After a long pause, he said abruptly, "The kids are dead."

Moses explored readiness for other deaths: "I justify myself because I'm taking risks myself, and I'm not asking people to do things I'm not willing to do. . . . If for any reason you're hesitant about what you're getting into, it's better for you to leave." He nearly begged them to go home, recorded one volunteer, and closed with a special plea to those going forward in the second wave, most of whom had trained as teachers to open the experimental Freedom Schools. "Be patient with the kids and with Mississippi," he said. "Because there is a distinction between being slow and being stupid. And the kids in Mississippi are very, very . . . very slow."

Moses withdrew to compose statements for the next day: a ringing defense of the summer project* and a passionate request that untrained sympathizers stay out of Mississippi. The volunteers started a slow movement song, "They say that freedom is a constant struggle." Boarding buses, they rolled south from Ohio in the darkness so that they, like Louise Hermey and Andrew Goodman the week before, could be dropped off at appointed stations in Mississippi before sundown on Saturday. By then, FBI Inspector [Joseph] Sullivan extended the systematic search of Neshoba County with grappling hooks and a small armada of skiffs to drag a fifty-mile stretch of the Pearl River.

---

* " . . . We are fully committed to continuing the Summer Project. This does not mean that we will attempt to provoke the state. . . . We are specifically avoiding any demonstrations for integrated facilities, as we do not feel the state is ready to permit such activity at this time. All workers, staff and Summer Volunteers alike, are pledged to non-violence in all situations."

Outside the 1964 Democratic National Convention, flanked by placards honoring civil rights martyrs Andrew Goodman, James Chaney, and Michael Schwerner (*left to right*), King exhorts delegates to seat the Mississippi Freedom Democratic Party.

— CHAPTER TEN —

Party Realignment: The Cow Palace and Atlantic City, 1964

The ongoing drama of Mississippi Freedom Summer coincided with final passage of the historic 1964 Civil Rights Act and with both presidential nominating conventions. The three missing civil rights workers turned up corpses in August, victims of a Klan lynching arranged by local officials. These overlapping events were intense, with racial politics flushed to the surface. The major parties confronted a looming shift in identity.

Most congressional Republicans voted for the civil rights bill. This was no surprise, inasmuch as the GOP "Party of Lincoln" had been associated with Negro advancement since its establishment just before the Civil War. However, the leading Republican presidential candidate broke with his party. After legal consultations with two future Supreme Court nominees—William Rehnquist and Robert Bork—Senator Barry Goldwater announced that he would oppose the bill as a usurpation of states' rights. This maverick stance made Goldwater an instant hero in the South, where Republican converts sprang up to challenge the one-party hegemony of Democrats. Goldwater pioneers developed an ingenious antifederal vocabulary to anchor conservative politics for a future without segregation.

The Democrats gathered next in Atlantic City, New Jersey. Nine months after the Kennedy assassination, President Lyndon Johnson nearly came undone over the fate of traditional all-white delegations. Needing Southern states to win, he harbored prominent Democrats who openly defected to Goldwater, but he also promised integrationist reform to challengers from Mississippi led by Bob Moses. Although Johnson would win the presidential election by a landslide, with Democrats ascendant in Congress, his compromise antagonized both political flanks.

Overall, the 1964 election marked an unprecedented shift in the structure of national politics. A partisan reversal would take hold over decades, driven and yet muffled by race, tainting the word "liberal" in both parties.

[From *Pillar of Fire*, pp. 401–6, 456–76, 493]

Republicans opened their national convention in the San Francisco Cow Palace [on] Monday, July 13. All three television networks covered the four-day national pageant more or less continuously, anticipating an abrupt regional and ideological shift of power toward Senator Goldwater's Western conservatives from the long-dominant Eastern business interests. . . . Hostilities erupted on the convention floor. Afterward, neither the triumphant Goldwater conservatives nor the defeated Rockefeller-Scranton liberals smoothed their raging antagonism in the interest of party unity. "Hell, I don't want to talk to that son-of-a-bitch," Goldwater growled when New York's Governor Nelson Rockefeller called to concede. *Life* magazine bemoaned the "ugly tone" of the entire convention.* The *New York Times* called it a "disaster" for both the United States and the Republicans, saying the Goldwater nomination could "reduce a once great party to the status of an ugly, angry, frustrated faction.". . .

Newsweek pronounced the San Francisco convention "stunningly total—and unconditional . . . an authentic party revolution, born of deep-seated frustration with the existing order, executed by a new breed of pros with a ruthless skill." Other mainstream outlets speculated about Eisenhower, the rejection of Wall Street Republicans, or Goldwater's poor prospects against Lyndon Johnson, but their excitements were mild beside the acute distress of Negro publications. "GOP Convention Spurns Negroes," cried the *Cleveland Call and Post.* "Negro Delegates to GOP Convention Suffer Week of Humiliation," headlined the Associated Negro Press newswire. "The Great Purge of Negroes," announced *Jet.* "GOP Negroes Washed Away by the Goldwater Ocean," said the *Chicago Defender.* Their focus was less on the Goldwater nomination itself than on the institutional rejection of cherished Republican fixtures such as George W. Lee of Memphis, delegate to every GOP convention since 1940, who had "seconded the nomination of Robert A. Taft" in 1952. The San Francisco convention,

---

* "It was a gathering of the utterly comfortable, come together to protest that they should be having it better . . . angry even in victory."

sweeping aside Lee's credentials claim that he and two hundred "regular" Negro Republicans had been railroaded out of the Shelby County caucus, seated "lily-white" delegations in Tennessee and every other Southern state "for the first time since Reconstruction Days," reported the *Pittsburgh Courier*, noting that the caucus of Southern Republicans, "to add insult to injury," named its hotel headquarters Fort Sumter. Southern Republicans re-formed as a homogeneous group. Of the region's 375 convention delegates, all were white and at least 366 supported Goldwater.

Minority observers mourned the loss of Republican stalwarts far beyond the sinecures* and patronage posts of the South. In "Cal. GOP/ White Man's Party," the *California Eagle* of Los Angeles protested a seldom-mentioned fact about Goldwater's victory over Rockefeller in the decisive June 2 primary: it gained convention seats and control of party machinery for a slate of eighty-six California delegates that "by deliberate choice" was exclusively white. Nationwide, by slating no Negro candidates and defeating most opposing tickets, Goldwater strategists whittled the number of Negro delegates to a minuscule fourteen of 1,308, roughly one per hundred, in what newspapers called the fewest "ever to be certified to a Republican convention."

At the Cow Palace, the rolling invective that startled television viewers fell personally upon this tiny remnant. The *Cleveland Call and Post* reported that George Fleming of New Jersey ran from the hall in tears, saying Negro delegates "had been shoved, pushed, spat on, and cursed with a liberal sprinkling of racial epithets." George Young, labor secretary of Pennsylvania, complained that Goldwater delegates harassed him to the point of setting his suit jacket on fire with a cigarette. Baseball legend Jackie Robinson summarized his "unbelievable hours" as an observer on the convention floor: "I now believe I know how it felt to be a Jew in Hitler's Germany."...

Neither established experts nor shell-shocked Negro Republicans anticipated a wholesale switch of party identification down to the roots of congressional and local offices. Historic affiliations were too well fixed, with Republicans more united behind Negro rights than Democrats. In Con-

---

* "The Georgia delegation," recalled a Cleveland paper, "for many years was headed by the first Negro national committeeman in either party, Henry Lincoln Johnson."

gress, fully 80 percent of House Republicans and 82 percent of GOP senators had just voted *for* the civil rights bill, with Democrats lagging behind because of their entrenched segregationist wing. In precincts and state conventions, Republicans everywhere were organized in part around the glorious memory of Emancipation, which was precisely what had reduced them to near extinction among Southerners. For generations, none but the occasional eccentric Republican had bothered to contest elections for Southern statehouses, legislatures, or courthouse jobs. Of forty-one U.S. representatives from the core Deep South states of Georgia, Alabama, Mississippi, Louisiana, and South Carolina, Republicans in 1964 numbered zero.

The century's first handful of promising Deep South Republican candidates arrived at the San Francisco convention hopeful of novel success in the fall elections. . . . Barry Goldwater had courted [South Carolina Senator Strom] Thurmond secretly . . . not merely to endorse him for president across partisan lines but to "go all the way and change parties." On September 16, Thurmond accomplished the switch in a statewide television address of slashing boldness. "The Democratic Party has abandoned the people . . .," he declared in the first of twenty-two bullet-like paragraphs on his former party as consummate evil: "The Democratic Party has invaded the private lives of people . . . has succored and assisted our Communist enemies . . . worships at the throne of power and materialism . . . has protected the Supreme Court in a reign of judicial tyranny." Thurmond proclaimed the November election a fulcrum of the ages: "The party of our fathers is dead. Those who took its name are engaged in another Reconstruction." Should Democrats prevail, he warned, "freedom as we have known it in this country is doomed." . . .

Martin Luther King and others denounced the Republican ticket on its first official day and nearly every day thereafter. With a peculiar mix of vehemence and care, King took pains to stop short of partisan endorsement, hoping that a sound enough defeat for Goldwater might restrain both parties from political white flight. . . .

Atlantic City . . . hosted a great storm of Democrats also in transition. At a preconvention hearing on Friday, August 21, George Wallace hotly denounced national Democratic leaders as revolutionaries who "would sell the birthright of our nation" to install "an alien philosophy of government." Having arranged by recent state law to expunge President Johnson and his running mate from Alabama ballots in November, so that Wallace himself could allocate "Democratic" votes in the Electoral College (eventually to Goldwater), Wallace notified convention leaders that he cared little whether or not they unseated his Alabama delegation over this supercession of the party's nominees. "I'm not here to beg," he declared. Wallace demanded that national Democrats repeal the civil rights law, and foretold otherwise an "uprising" on par with the revolt against Reconstruction. Against an excess of "central authority, given free reign by this very party," he promised a conservative movement to "take charge of one of the parties in the next four years.". . .

On Saturday afternoon, the Mississippi Freedom Democratic Party (MFDP) challengers filed into seats directly across from the opposing Mississippi regulars. "We have only an hour to tell you a story of tragedy and terror in Mississippi," lawyer Joe Rauh began. He faced the Credentials Committee as a comfortable peer, owning one of its 110 votes himself as a delegate from the District of Columbia. . . . Rauh summoned . . . Fannie Lou Hamer, who limped forward on her polio-damaged left hip to place her purse on the witness table as attendants pinned a microphone to her cotton dress. Hamer launched her story. . . . She recalled an incident in Winona from the first commotion ("I stepped off the bus to see what was happening") to the steadily approaching dread in jail. "I began to hear the sounds of licks and screams," Hamer testified. ". . . I was carried out of that cell into another cell where they had two Negro prisoners. The State Highway Patrolman ordered the first Negro to take the blackjack." Then, near the end of her allotted eight minutes, Hamer vanished from television screens. "We will return to this scene in Atlantic City," said correspondent Edwin Newman from a control desk, "but now we switch to the White House and NBC's Robert Goralski."

President Johnson . . . mounted a diversion with the cooperation of news outlets massed on alert for revelation of his vice presidential choice.

He stepped before White House correspondents, with several governors in tow, and stretched the moment with a sympathetic reference to [Texas Governor John] Connally—still suffering from rifle wounds inflicted in the Dallas motorcade—noting that "on this day nine months ago at very nearly this same hour in the afternoon, the duties of this office were thrust upon me by a terrible moment in our national history." The President ducked questions and withdrew to the governors' conclave in the East Room, leaving reporters with material for unrequited headlines: "Johnson Still Silent About Running Mate."

Knocked off camera, the Atlantic City hearing concluded with four more MFDP witnesses. After Rita Schwerner, for whom a section of spectators stood in silent tribute, Rauh called the national leaders James Farmer of CORE and Roy Wilkins of the NAACP, then King for a summary exhortation. "I say to you that any party in the world should be proud to have a delegation such as this seated in their midst," said King. "For it is in these saints in ordinary walks of life that the true spirit of democracy finds its most profound and abiding expression." With a glance to the Mississippi regulars at the opposite table, he bemoaned a state party that since the last Democratic convention had forced the dispatch of twenty thousand troops before it yielded "a single Negro into a state university," and was "already pledged to defy the candidate and platform of this great national body." King testified that Mississippi was "no mean issue" in world affairs—not "for all the disfranchised millions of this earth, whether they be in Mississippi or Alabama, behind the Iron Curtain, floundering in the mire of South African apartheid, or freedom-seeking persons in Cuba who have now gone three years without election. Recognition of the Freedom Democratic Party would say to them that somewhere in this world there is a nation that cares about justice." . . .

Evening news broadcasts delivered Hamer to larger audiences than Johnson had preempted in the afternoon. Atlantic City's Western Union office reported 416 night telegrams supporting the MFDP, against only one for the regulars, and Rauh claimed that his "knockout" witnesses "won the Boardwalk." Observing that President Johnson knew above all else how to count votes, he relished the bargaining ahead. "We won't take any of those second-rate compromises," Rauh told reporters Saturday night. . . .

When party chairman John Bailey tried to congratulate him for the "good start" in Atlantic City, [President] Johnson glumly predicted that the Mississippi roll call must come that [Tuesday] night and that "every one of those big states will have to go with the Negroes." Bailey confirmed that his native New England delegations would likely vote three to one for the MFDP minority report ("they don't like Mississippi"). Johnson said the victorious Negro coalition was digging its own grave. "I think they're bigger than the President this morning," he told Bailey, "and I think it's just water on Goldwater's paddle."

He disclosed a new plan that morning to his Texas rancher friend, Judge A. W. Moursund. When Press Secretary George Reedy called for instructions before the midday briefing, Johnson read to him from a statement in progress—the first one drafted by his own hand in twenty years—announcing his intention not to run.* He told Reedy the convention could nominate "a new and fresh fellow." His voice trailed off.

Reedy let the silence hang. "This would throw the nation in quite an uproar, sir," he said quietly.

The President called his chief aide Walter Jenkins in Atlantic City. "If anybody's entitled to know, you are," he said. He repeated his suspicion that the MFDP was "born in the Justice Department" as a creature of Robert Kennedy. "I don't believe there'll be many attacks on the orders I issued on Tonkin Gulf if I'm not a candidate," said Johnson. He tearfully described fears of a breakdown. "I don't want to be in this place like Wilson†," he said, "and I do not believe I can physically and mentally carry the responsibilities of the bomb and the world and the nigras and the South and so forth." When Jenkins gently doubted he would go through with it, the President insisted that he would—sometime after his foreign policy lunch.

Lady Bird Johnson endured all through Tuesday the depressed side of her husband's distemper—wide-eyed silence under the covers for naps, shades

---

* "... The times require leadership about which there is no doubt and a voice that men of all parties, sections, and color can follow. I have learned after trying very hard that I am not that voice or that leader. Therefore ..."

† Johnson referred to President Woodrow Wilson, who suffered a debilitating stroke in 1920.

drawn from the daylight. "I do not remember hours I ever found harder," she would write in her memoirs, and at the time she wrote out for him her anguished appeal: "Beloved—You are as brave a man as Harry Truman—or FDR—or Lincoln. You can go on to find some peace, some achievement amidst all the pain. . . . To step out now would be wrong for your country, and I see nothing but a lonely wasteland for your future. Your friends would be frozen in embarrassed silence and your enemies jeering. . . . I know it's only *your* choice. . . . I love you always, Bird."

Everyone else prepared blindly for the decisive crunch in Atlantic City. . . . At a midday mass meeting, exhausted MFDP partisans rallied . . . to hold out for their fallback position of shared seats with the regulars. Their lawyer, Rauh, charged to bargain for nothing less, was intercepted outside the Credentials Committee with a peremptory message to call Walter Reuther. "The convention has decided," Reuther told him sharply. He disclosed two new concessions: Aaron Henry and Edwin King of the MFDP would be seated as voting delegates at large, and the party would establish a special commission to enforce nondiscrimination standards for the 1968 convention. Reuther emphasized that Johnson was holding out for a basic party loyalty oath for Mississippi as well as Alabama; no delegate could vote without signing one. "This is a tremendous victory," he said. "I want you to go in there and accept it." If he refused, Reuther promised to terminate Rauh's employment as Washington counsel for the United Auto Workers. . . .

Frantic knocks and cries of "It's over!" pulled the negotiators from the bedroom to behold the commotion around the suite's television set, on which [Senator Walter] Mondale was presenting the Mississippi compromise to reporters as a finished deal. "You cheated!" shrieked Moses, whirling to accuse Senator Hubert Humphrey and Reuther of sham talks as a diversionary trick. The MFDP leaders stalked out with King to their meeting place in the basement of Union Temple Baptist, and the remnant that converged there from the Credentials Committee walked into pandemonium. Questions flew about a "fix," whose most treacherous and paralyzing effect seemed to be a cascading rumor that the MFDP had accepted the compromise already. There was talk of setups, especially against negotiating brokers such as Rauh, who recalled that Moses flinched from the trapdoor settlement as from "a white man hitting him with a whip.". . .

The unexpected breakthrough revived President Johnson until he heard from the two leading moderates who had been rallying Southerners for him at the convention. Together, governors Carl Sanders of Georgia and John Connally of Texas called Tuesday afternoon to warn of "a wholesale walkout from the South." Sanders himself threatened to leave and take the Georgia delegation with him. Johnson, having despaired for a month that Humphrey and Reuther could prevent a roll call victory for the MFDP, recoiled from sudden ambush on the other flank. Exasperated, he demanded to know how the MFDP's two "symbolic" at-large delegates could hurt anybody when they did not reduce the vote of the all-white delegation. "Mississippi's got every vote they ever had," said the President. "Georgia's got every vote they ever had. And we're not gonna *have* any votes to begin with!"

"I'm telling you because you want me to tell you the truth," Sanders declared. "It looks like we're turning the Democratic party over to the nigras. . . ." Martin Luther King was deciding who could be a delegate, he said. "It's gonna cut our throats from ear to ear."

Johnson argued that the MFDP really deserved representation in Mississippi itself. "Pistols kept 'em out," he said heatedly. "These people went in and begged to go into the conventions. They've got half the population, and they won't let 'em. They lock 'em out."

"They're not registered," Sanders insisted.

Johnson's temper fell into quiet pronouncement. "You and I just can't survive our political modern life," he said, "with these goddamn fellas down there that are eatin' 'em for breakfast every morning. They have got to quit that. And they got to let 'em vote, and let 'em shave, and let 'em eat, and things like that. And they don't do it.". . .

Press Secretary Reedy hesitantly answered a summons to the presidential quarters when the convention broadcasts signed off about midnight Tuesday. From considerable experience, he hoped the morning's resignation vow was forgotten, but he found Johnson in renewed despair over the threat of demonstrations and Southern walkouts. "By God, I'm gonna go up there and quit," said Johnson. "Fuck 'em all."

Reedy slathered on reassurances, lumbering after Johnson on one of his hyperkinetic walks around the White House South Lawn. He said the President did not need to go to Atlantic City until Thursday, once he was nominated and the convention safely in his pocket. He pleaded with Johnson not to hand the country to Goldwater. Johnson merely said that he was having trouble with his withdrawal statement and ordered Reedy to draft it. When Reedy refused, the President flayed him as an incompetent, disloyal tormentor. Reedy ended the ordeal only by promising to write something, but the predawn resignation he typed out was his own.

On Wednesday morning, the MFDP delegation regathered amidst second thoughts about the compromise and rumors that the administration might relax some of the insulting details. Rauh told his friend Senator Humphrey that "the dumb bastards on your side—and I'm sure it wasn't you, Hubert—chose our two people instead of letting them choose their own two people." Humphrey dragged himself back to work, saying he was so battered that "I honestly don't care too much anymore" about Johnson's test for vice president, and Rauh joined a phalanx of speakers at Union Temple Baptist. He urged the delegates to reconsider the compromise, as did Senator Wayne Morse and Aaron Henry. Bayard Rustin argued that they must broaden their outlook from moral protest to political alliance, during which Mendy Samstein of SNCC jumped up to shout, "You're a traitor, Bayard!" . . .

Martin Luther King delivered a speech of formal neutrality. "I am not going to counsel you to accept or reject," he said. "That is your decision." He balanced a denunciation of Johnson's remote-control mistreatment against the leavening hope for political progress, airing his conflicted private advice: "So, being a Negro leader, I want you to take this, but if I were a Mississippi Negro, I would vote against it." The delegates gave King generous applause on both sides. Some were still pinching themselves that all the big shots were worked up over their decision, and some shared the distaste of the student movement for King's straddling.

Bob Moses swayed nearly all of them against the compromise. "We're not here to bring politics to our morality," he said, "but to bring morality to our politics." One admirer said, "Moses could have been Socrates or Aristotle. . . . I mean he tore King up." When the outsiders departed after the speeches, a few MFDP delegates ventured praise of the compromise as "getting somewhere," but the larger voices—especially Victoria Gray, Annie Devine, and Fannie Lou Hamer—scorned it as a paltry temptation. . . . The delegates voted again to reject the Democratic offer. "We didn't come all this way for no two seats," said Hamer.

Meanwhile, Walter Reuther left for Washington to deliver a report in the West Hallway outside President Johnson's bedroom. No record survives of their eighty minutes alone, nor of Johnson's initial state of mind after the serial crises, but Reuther's bracing news . . . accented the positive. There was no residual chance for a roll call on Mississippi. The *Washington Post* predicted that the "vast bulk" of Southern delegates would stay on, and praised Johnson as the invisible wizard who helped the Democratic party "finally rid itself of the divisive civil rights issue which has plagued every national convention beginning with 1948."

The President buzzed for his press secretary after Reuther departed, but Reedy, cringing with his own undelivered resignation, ducked three calls before learning that Johnson was racing forward again. . . . Johnson announced Humphrey within hours, in person, to a pleasantly astonished convention that swept them jointly to nomination. The nominees returned to give acceptance speeches at the closing session Thursday night. . . . An unbroken wave of applause lasted fully twenty-two minutes when Robert Kennedy introduced the film about his brother with Shakespeare's tribute to Romeo: "When he shall die/Take him and cut him out in little stars/And he will make the face of heaven so fine/That all the world will be in love with night/And pay no worship to the garish sun." Johnson by then could welcome, even absorb, some of the outpouring as the secure successor to President Kennedy. . . .

Bob Moses and six others stood vigil in an aisle through the Kennedy tribute Thursday night, wearing black neck placards embossed with JFK's silhouette and his exhortation, "Ask not what your country. . . ." Moses was among many who already felt Atlantic City a bitter turning point for the Mississippi movement, if not for all of American politics. Outside, Fannie Lou Hamer led farewell choruses of "We Shall Overcome," and fireworks from President Johnson's gigantic fifty-sixth birthday celebration illuminated the whole Boardwalk, including portraits of Mississippi martyrs held aloft.

King leaves a strange and inconclusive truce meeting with FBI Director
J. Edgar Hoover on December 1, 1964.

— CHAPTER ELEVEN —

King, J. Edgar Hoover, and the Nobel Peace Prize, 1964

The legendary gulf between King and FBI Director Hoover was
largely concealed from public view. Not until 1969, a year after King's
death, did testimony at the draft evasion trial of boxer Muhammad
Ali disclose that the FBI had wiretapped King under a 1963 order
signed by Attorney General Robert Kennedy. Not until the mid-1970s,

after Hoover's death in 1972, did congressional investigations reveal voluminous evidence of the FBI's clandestine hostility to King and the larger civil rights movement—wiretaps, bugs, propaganda, and harassments known in FBI jargon as Counter-Intelligence Program (COINTELPRO).

In retrospect, the FBI's massive campaign was hardly surprising. Through a long reign as its founding director (since 1924), Hoover had made his FBI the most insular and autocratic agency of domestic government. Into the 1960s, the only Negro FBI agents were a handful of butlers and chauffeurs in personal service to him. Conflict was inevitable by then, as Director Hoover's homogeneous, finely tuned hierarchy confronted a freedom movement dedicated to broadening and fulfilling democratic norms.

Hoover's personal disdain for King flared once into public controversy, at a crucial turning point for both men. In mid-November 1964, Hoover was a few weeks from the mandatory federal retirement age of seventy, and President Johnson, who alone could arrange an exemption, had just won landslide reelection. Hoover provoked a scandal that tested his popular support and the intimidating factor of his secret FBI files against a president at peak political strength.

Hoover launched the character assault just after King had been designated to receive the Nobel Peace Prize in December. The attack heightened King's crisis of doubt and self-worth for the great honor. Always ambitious, he disappointed staff advisers eager to bask for years in the demise of legal segregation. Having been a reluctant leader at times, he went resolutely from the Oslo ceremonies to mount a campaign for voting rights in Selma, Alabama, and soon back to jail. King would intensify his pursuit of nonviolent witness repeatedly thereafter, downward into lonelier causes until he wound up among the sanitation workers of Memphis.

[From *Pillar of Fire*, pp. 526–33, 540–47]

On the following day, Wednesday, November 18, [1964,] Hoover gave a rare press briefing—his first in many years, the first ever with exclusively female reporters—to a maverick offshoot of the Women's National Press Club. Because women were barred (until 1971) from membership in the National Press Club, pioneers had formed the WNPC, and because most members of the Women's National Press Club specialized in traditional ladies' features on family or fashion, the Hoover interview fell to an informal club called the McLendon Press Group, founded by Texas reporter Sarah McLendon. Some members, including one soon to be fired for saying she expected no hard news, shied away from the anticipated spy lecture as so much "male shadowboxing," but eighteen reporters filed into the imposing Director's office furnished with a new silver coffee urn and lamp fixtures in the shape of pistols.

Hoover talked nearly three times his allotted hour. When his monologue on FBI history slowed toward possible questions, he called for the FBI annual report and read excerpts with biting asides. . . . He expressed frustration that "in spite of some remarkable success in civil rights cases, some detractors alleged the FBI has done nothing in this field." Hoover indignantly recalled Martin Luther King's complaints about FBI performance in Albany, Georgia, during 1962, which the Director attributed to a misguided belief that FBI agents were native Southerners. "In view of King's attitude and his continued criticism of the FBI on this point," said Hoover, "I consider King to be the most notorious liar in the country."

FBI Assistant Director Deke DeLoach, fearing a public relations disaster, passed Hoover several notes suggesting that the "liar" comment be placed off the record along with Hoover's assertions that King was "one of the lowest characters in the country" and "controlled" by Communist advisers, but Hoover rebuffed any notion of retraction. "The girls," DeLoach would testify eleven years later, "could hardly wait to leave to get to the telephone." No such story had been broken by female journalists alone, and more than a few male news staffs tried to mask their secondhand accounts of the women's interview behind a different interpretation. ("Hoover Assails Warren Findings," announced the *New York Times*, and the *Washington Post* headlined his "Blast at Police Corruption.") Nevertheless, the "notorious liar" charge exploded above such distractions.

Vacationing in Bimini with King, Andrew Young knew something big had struck when helicopters chartered by reporters began landing. In New York, the first radio bulletins about the "notorious liar" statement broke up a research committee meeting on plans for the Nobel Prize trip. . . . In Washington, Acting Attorney General Nicholas Katzenbach walked into Hoover's office. "I couldn't be more unhappy," the Director declared before Katzenbach said a word. "Never should have done it. Never should have seen all those women reporters. DeLoach got me into it." In a preemptive monologue, Hoover said he of course had to tell the truth about King once DeLoach trapped him into a foolish predicament. A despairing Katzenbach went directly to the White House. . . . Inside the FBI, agents and officials massed behind Hoover as though it were King who had initiated the attack. By late Thursday night, the Atlanta office compiled a review of all past dealings since "the freedom rides in the summer of sixty [*sic*]," under counterpoint headings—"King States," answered by "Facts"—to buttress Hoover's charge that King was a liar. . . . One-way intercepts allowed headquarters to make the worst of rattled private opinions. Wiretaps picked up King telling Rev. C. T. Vivian that Hoover "is old and getting senile." Bureau supervisors pounced on wiretap intelligence that Rustin wanted King to seek Hoover's replacement, calling such behavior "further evidence" of subversion "in line with a long-held communist objective, to launch a campaign to oust the Director as head of the FBI." Hoover scrawled a response on Friday's memo recommending that he neither dignify King's [peace-seeking] telegram with a reply nor justify his own conduct further:

> O.K. But I don't understand why we are unable to get the true facts before the public. We can't even get our accomplishments published. We are never taking the aggressive, but allow lies to remain unanswered.

"Being handled—11/20/64," DeLoach wrote next to Hoover's comment. Propaganda operations expanded clandestinely to more reporters, to religious groups, and to civic leaders. Agents rushed the first new batch of anti-King material to other government agencies by Sunday, the first anniversary of the Kennedy assassination, and assembled even before then a "highlight" recording of bugged sex groans and party jokes, together with a contrived anonymous letter calling King "a great liability for all of us Negroes." The letter to King warned that "your end is approaching," and concluded, "You are done. There is but one way out for you. You better take it before your filthy, abnormal fraudulent self is bared to the nation." FBI specialists combined the highlight recording with the letter, and moved what became known as the suicide package at a lightning pace for government work on a weekend—through bureaucratic approval, technical selection, composition, air shipment via courier, and finally mail drop to King from Miami (in order to camouflage its Washington origin)—all by Saturday night, November 21. . . .

Advisers gathered somberly in King's [New York Barbizon Hotel] room on Wednesday night, November 25, with the returned vacationers Abernathy, Bernard Lee, and Andrew Young in pajamas to receive the New Yorkers: Clarence Jones, Bayard Rustin, noted psychologist Kenneth Clark, labor leader Cleveland Robinson, and lawyer Harry Wachtel. Was Hoover acting for Johnson or not? What did Hoover know? What did he want? . . .

"Trilogy" emerged from the meeting as shorthand for the three arenas of vulnerability in surveillance politics: money, loyalty, and sex. The most devastating of the three was presumed to be money corruption—slush funds, tax fraud, hidden wealth, charities fleeced for private gain—but here King said he was happy to prove himself innocent again as in his 1960 trial, no matter how much snooping the FBI did. As for the protracted struggle over the taint of Communism, the prevailing view was that the movement had behaved too defensively already. Rather than retreat further, King talked of restoring his friendship with Stanley Levison. On the matter of his private life, however, King conceded vaguely that there were "things that could be exploited." He was squeamish about revealing himself to his white friend Wachtel, and privately enlisted his aides to keep the admission from filtering back to Levison, but the puzzling emergency drove King to seek Wachtel's judgment about Hoover.

Wachtel offered advice from his experience in the corporate world. He saw Hoover as an entrenched chief executive who had sounded off impulsively and now needed a face-saving escape. "If you were one of my clients," Wachtel told King, he would recommend that he arrange a meeting at which Hoover could vent his criticism over King's lifestyle, and then "maybe you and he can issue a statement that you've had a fruitful discussion." This proposal aroused a chorus of dissent from the other advisers, who saw Hoover as an enemy who gave no quarter. . . .

Years later, a number of prominent correspondents acknowledged being pitched by DeLoach and his staff with anti-King briefings on sex and skullduggery. From pay phones and self-conscious trysts, reporters at the time circulated tidbits among government and movement sources, massaging reactions toward an attributable story, and Attorney General Katzenbach himself undertook to trace the Thanksgiving rumors. He called in Ben Bradlee of *Newsweek*, who refused on principle to name DeLoach as his source, and DeLoach, who flatly denied that the FBI leaked anything. This dead-end matched Katzenbach's experience in the Justice Department. In order to investigate leaks, he could call only upon the FBI, and FBI reports always categorically defended the Bureau itself.* . . . Frustrated and angry, Katzenbach took the extraordinary step of presenting his alarm directly to President Johnson on Saturday, November 28, at the LBJ Ranch in Texas. With Burke Marshall, Katzenbach put forward his conviction that the FBI was peddling anti-King poison all over Washington and beyond, that DeLoach was lying about it with brazen impunity, that Hoover was out of touch, bordering on senile, and that the circus of impropriety was especially dangerous now because of breaks in the Mississippi murder case. . . .

---

* "Their defense is always that it must have come from somebody in your office," Katzenbach wryly stated in a 1969 oral history. ". . . You get back thirty seconds later: they made a complete full field investigation [and] it was not leaked by anybody in the FBI. [*Laughter.*] And they had positive evidence that it was not. But of course they run that whole operation there."

Johnson's private calculation on whether to fire Hoover was direct: "I'd rather have him inside the tent pissing out than outside pissing in." This quip reflected Johnson's estimate of their relative standing in the press. Like other presidents since Calvin Coolidge, who had first appointed the FBI Director, Johnson instinctively chose to side with Hoover against reporters rather than with reporters against Hoover. He ordered his staff to warn the FBI that Bradlee of *Newsweek* was not a reliable outlet for confidential information, which of course betrayed Katzenbach's brief and sent Hoover only the subtlest notice that the President was personally aware of his scurrilous "battle of personalities.". . .

King flew from London to Oslo on December 8. Norway's King Olaf V sent for him and Coretta the next afternoon, and received them in private audience at the Royal Palace. There was considerable tension within the King group, which had swelled to thirty people. . . . Outside the Grand Hotel, officers directed King and Coretta to the limousine with Nobel Committee chairman Gunnar Jahn, and others to the line of cars waiting behind a press barricade. Ralph and Juanita Abernathy requested to ride along in car number one, which pitted them against the Norwegian protocol chief. An argument ensued, with the Abernathys insisting that they always rode with the Kings and the protocol chief standing firm with her calligraphied manifest. Abernathy appealed to King, who stood frozen with embarrassment, then tried to push his way past the security officers. From behind, friends pleaded with Abernathy that there were plenty of limousines in the motorcade. By the time the Abernathys were removed to their assigned car, Andrew Young and Bernard Lee refused to ride with them. They walked the short distance to the ceremony through the December cold, talking over anew the mystery of King's attachment to Abernathy. . . .

King returned the next evening to deliver his formal Nobel lecture at Oslo University, where a standing-room crowd included several hundred students carrying Viking torches. Again he used his own handwritten draft with few modifications. He omitted sentences scribbled in his margins, such as "war is the most extreme externalization of an inner violence of the spirit," and inserted several less abstract ideas suggested by Rustin and Wachtel, including a paragraph welcoming the defeat of Goldwater in the American election. From Gandhi's India through postcolonial Africa to the American South, said King, "the freedom movement is spreading the widest liberation in human history," and he recommended the discipline of nonviolence "for study and for serious experimentation in every field of human conflict, by no means excluding the relations between nations."

He had added sections on poverty and war to his reflections on racial oppression. "All that I have said," King concluded, "boils down to the point of affirming that mankind's survival is dependent upon man's ability to solve the problems of racial injustice, poverty and war; the solution of these problems is in turn dependent upon man squaring his moral progress with his scientific process, and learning the practical art of living in harmony." Proclaiming new opportunity for "the shirtless and barefoot people" and hope for "a dark confused world," King pronounced the era "a great time to be alive. Therefore, I am not yet discouraged about the future." He had inserted the word "yet" between the lines of his handwritten draft as a late change. . . .

King arrived in New York to a whirlwind on December 17 . . . [to] a tumultuous night rally at Harlem's 369th Artillery Armory, on 142nd Street. . . . He wrestled out loud with pressures to grasp sweet renown in the larger world. For ten days he had been "talking with kings and queens, meeting and talking with prime ministers of nations," King said. "That isn't the usual pattern of my life, to have people saying nice things about me. Oh, this is a marvelous mountaintop. I wish I could stay here tonight. But the valley calls me."

Six days earlier in Oslo, addressing what he called "man's ethical infantilism," King had used the Greek myth of Ulysses to illustrate his belief that it was better to overcome the siren music of evil by listening to the melodies of Orpheus than by stuffing wax into one's ears. Now he preached in the Harlem armory on his favorite biblical parable of the rich man Dives, condemned because he never noticed the humble beggar Lazarus outside his door. King did not mention his resolve to go straight to Selma, but six times he tore himself from the mountain. "Oh, there are some humble people down in the valley!" he cried, in his distinctive mix of despair and inspiration. ". . . I go back with a faith that the wheels of the gods grind slowly but exceedingly fine," he said. "I go back with a faith that you shall reap what you sow. With that faith, I go back to the valley."

March 21, 1965: Voting rights demonstrators cross the Edmund Pettus Bridge, beginning a third and final attempt to march from Selma to Montgomery.

— CHAPTER TWELVE —

Crossroads in Selma, 1965

Bob Moses, overburdened by raw politics and deaths in his wake, hushed a SNCC conference by passing around a block of cheese and jug of wine. "I want you to eat and drink," he said. "Some of you need to leave." He told disjointed personal stories. His SNCC brothers and sisters were becoming creatures of the media, he warned, contending for power, and the nation would take fifty years to come to its senses over race. He vanished after announcing that his last name no longer would be Moses.

In Alabama, King aimed to build upon long-suffering witness by student-led SNCC projects for the right to vote, which had grown slowly into the Mississippi Freedom Summer of 1964. His Selma campaign followed the pattern of Birmingham's showdown over segregation two years earlier. Once again, careful planning and bold demonstrations led to harsh repression with negligible results. The outside world scarcely noticed another King manifesto—"There are more Negroes in jail with me than there are on the voting rolls"—nor the unprecedented march of voteless Negro schoolteachers, holding up toothbrushes, from their classrooms to jail. The national press ignored even a surprise visit by Malcolm X, days before his own assassination, during which King's colleagues, fearful of incendiary scorn for non-violence, were astonished to hear Malcolm address Selma's battered marchers in soothing tribute: "I pray that all the fear that has ever been in your heart will be taken out."

As in Birmingham, setbacks and attrition pushed King to desperate measures at the brink of failure. There were marches from churches to rural courthouses outside Selma, met with locked doors and violence under the cover of darkness. Late in February, when young marcher Jimmie Lee Jackson died of gunshot wounds inflicted by an Alabama state trooper, an overwrought James Bevel proposed a mass march fifty-four miles from Selma to petition Alabama's Governor George Wallace in Montgomery. "I must go see the king!" he cried from the pulpit, invoking the biblical mission of Esther to "request before him for her people." Nearly all movement leaders dismissed the notion as quixotic. Such marchers, while defying hostile state officials, would be exposed and vulnerable in overnight camps through Klan-dominated Lowndes County, where no Negro from its 70 percent majority had even tried to vote since 1900. King, however, reassessed another "crazy" Bevel idea from the standpoint of a minority's nonviolent quest to transform what was normal. He authorized the long march to leave Selma on Sunday, March 7, 1965.

The trek became an instant historical icon—"Bloody Sunday"— when news footage flashed around the world of Negroes beaten, trampled, and tear-gassed by Alabama troopers back across Selma's Edmund Pettus Bridge. The images, which still remain synonymous with U.S. democracy in crisis, lit the fuse for two weeks of concentrated drama and two more attempts to cross the bridge. The next try, twelve days before a perilous but triumphant finale, ensnarled King in perhaps his supreme test of balance as a movement leader in national politics.

This abortive "turnaround" march of March 9 made for poor television, and is largely forgotten. Behind the scenes, a storm of political forces lodged competing claims. Remarkably, from as far away as Hawaii, some eight hundred religious leaders had answered King's emergency appeal within forty-eight hours. They were already present and primed to share the risk, but U.S. District Judge Frank Johnson ordered King to halt pending a judicial inquiry. SNCC leaders, who had boycotted Sunday's march as reckless, converged in determination to march now regardless. President Johnson had sent two emissaries, Justice Department lawyer John Doar and former Florida Governor LeRoy Collins, to warn that any action to secure voting rights hinged on compliance with the federal courts. Governor Wallace, while vowing to crush any second march, debated trick strategies to lure an unprepared host into the primeval wilderness of Lowndes County.

Only two days after Bloody Sunday, conflicting agendas and predictions besieged King on all sides—from an inspired but fractious movement and branches of government at every level. Still undecided what to do, he led his reinforced lines toward barricades at the Selma city limit.

[From *At Canaan's Edge*, pp. 76–87, 100–10]

Silence and bright sunshine fell on the second march to crest the bridge high above the Alabama River, as though re-creating Sunday's instant history on a larger scale. More than twice as many blue helmets spanned Highway 80 on the flatland below, from a deployment to Selma that the local newspaper put at five hundred Alabama troopers. Major Cloud stood a short distance behind his previous position to accommodate some 150 foreign and domestic journalists who crowded along the shoulders, and again confronted the approaching lines with orders to disperse. King sparred briefly over rights, then secured from Cloud a brief truce for prayerful decision. The front ranks knelt at his beckoning, and a wave of dry-throated marchers sank slowly behind them for nearly a mile to six ambulances poised in the rear, far past earshot of Ralph Abernathy's public prayer—"We come to present our bodies as a living sacrifice. . . ." A few skeptics stood on lookout near the front, peeking. One bruised, blue-collar veteran of Sunday wore his construction helmet as a precaution.

Attorney General Katzenbach called the White House at 2:56 P.M. "We're at the critical moment," he told presidential aide Bill Moyers. "I'll keep you posted." Chain-smoking cigarettes at his desk, Katzenbach monitored a speakerphone connected by open line to John Doar. Noise crackled above static. "What's that applause?" asked Katzenbach.

"They're cheering the white women," Doar replied. Two dignitaries, initially held back in case of another preemptive charge by troopers, slowly made their way into the standoff on the arm of Rev. Farley Wheelwright. Newspapers would identify them as Mrs. Paul Douglas, wife of the Democratic senator from Illinois, and Mrs. Charles Tobey, widow of the late Republican senator from New Hampshire—both wearing dress gloves and hats, one in pearls. Tobey's daughter, psychiatrist Belinda Strait, had been among the medical volunteers overwhelmed on Sunday. "And now one of them is talking to King," Doar reported.

From another roadside telephone, on through concluding prayers by Bishop Lord and Rabbi Dresner, Colonel Lingo exchanged information and orders over an open line to Governor Wallace. As the marchers began to rise again from the pavement, some singing the movement standard "We Shall Overcome" and others easing forward with scattered cheers, Major Cloud executed a surprise maneuver. "Troopers, withdraw!" he shouted, and the officers swung back from the center of the road with their portable barricades. To the horror of bystanders Doar and Collins, the way to Montgomery lay open.

King stood stunned at the divide, with but an instant to decide whether this was a trap or a miraculous parting of the Red Sea. If he stepped ahead, the thrill of heroic redemption for Bloody Sunday could give way to any number of reversals—arrests, attacks, laughingstock exhaustion in hostile country—all with marchers compromised as flagrant transgressors of the federal order. If he stepped back, he could lose or divide the movement under a cloud of timidity. If he hesitated or failed, at least some of the marchers would surge through the corridor of blue uniforms toward their goal.

"We will go back to the church now!" shouted King, peeling around. Abernathy and the congressional wives fell in, as did James Farmer of the Congress of Racial Equality (CORE) and Rev. Robert Spike, head of the National Council of Churches' Commission on Religion and Race. Andrew Young stationed himself at the point to wave oncoming marchers into a turnaround loop. SNCC leaders James Forman and Silas Norman, who had moved ahead, wheeled to catch up from behind, utterly perplexed. From the roadside, Governor Collins remained petrified that a stray gunshot from angry whites or a runaway marcher could break the spell of disengagement. Doar exclaimed over the telephone that there was a switch, gaining momentum. "Now I'm sure," he told the Attorney General. "The crowd's turning back." Katzenbach called the White House with the news. FBI agents dryly notified headquarters that King retreated at 3:09 P.M., five minutes after greeting Mrs. Douglas.

Governor Collins was euphoric. "If I hadn't done anything else in my lifetime," the federal emissary would record a decade later, "I had something to feel good about." In Washington, Katzenbach numbly withdrew from the commotion of his own office to ponder the government's future stance toward the entangled parties. "Now I want to think about this awhile," he said. For those returning to Selma across Pettus Bridge, a geyser of emotion blended joy with rage. A Roman Catholic priest cried out, "Thank you, Lord." Tears welled up in some who felt spared recurrent terror, while others sobbed over the letdown from a transcendent moment. Rev. Edwin King, who had been jailed and beaten and defrocked for integration in Mississippi, cried fitfully over a U-turn he considered a disastrous waste of moral courage, and forever lost trust in Martin Luther King. James Forman and other SNCC leaders fretted about treachery and betrayal of an unprecedented nonviolent army that had been stoked to march or die. Silas Norman, having set aside his fear and strategic dissent to join this time, sagged with fresh humiliation for being swept along backward without knowing why, and vowed never again to march in Selma. Willie Ricks moaned over the suddenness, believing that with any preparation the SNCC organizers could have bolted past King to steal most of the march. When an elder cautioned that divided leadership was lethal for minorities, Ricks and others launched a spirited rendition of "Ain't Gonna Let Nobody Turn Me 'Round." Their sarcasm was well disguised by the metaphorical optimism of the traditional movement hymn as it wafted along the lines. . . .

James Reeb's name commanded national headlines on Wednesday morning, March 10. Details of the dramatic ambush—how the three ministers took a wrong turn in the dark past a reputed Klan hangout called the Silver Moon diner—eclipsed brooding controversies about the abbreviated march, and fresh cascades of emotion swelled the reaction to Sunday's televised violence. Of the many newcomers who filed into Brown Chapel that morning, one Catholic philosopher from Missouri's Fontbonne College was mystified to behold in the pulpit "a squat figure in blue jeans and a bizarre beanie," then guessed from the ensuing shower of parables and entertainment that "one of Martin Luther King's most articulate spokesmen" must be concealing himself in an outfit of "local color." James Bevel coached the crowd to sort through every proposed action for constructive purpose. "We are testifying," he said. "Remember that. Some people have a hard time understanding nonviolence." Bevel claimed an immense untapped power for the doctrine to break down barriers when people willing to suffer worked hard to frame questions of justice unambiguously. "If nonviolence can work in Alabama," he declared, "it can work in South Africa."

At 12:47 P.M., Rev. L. L. Anderson led the crowd of five hundred outside to a roadblock under a chinaberry tree less than a block down Sylvan Street, where Selma's Mayor Joseph Smitherman, backed by a line of policemen, declared a permanent blockade. "You can make all the statements you want," added Public Safety Director Wilson Baker, "but you are not going to march." Behind Baker, flanked by deputies and possemen, Sheriff Jim Clark wore a white helmet and his trademark button pledging "Never" to abandon segregation. Behind them formed a loose reserve of one hundred Alabama troopers.

Thus began a marathon standoff. Sister Antona, a Negro nun from St. Louis, was the first to take a bullhorn to deliver a simple statement about why she had made the journey. One by one, more than thirty speakers stepped forward for nearly two hours—a rabbi from New Jersey, a student from Yale, a priest from Minnesota. At four o'clock, when members of an ecumenical delegation headed home to Missouri in two chartered airplanes, they were such an instant phenomenon that the powerful St. Louis radio station KMOX put Sister Antona and five other "nuns of Selma" directly on the air with stories that drew a flood of more than twenty thousand phone calls. Listeners from forty states variously praised them as national saviors and denounced them for perverting their image of a nun's cloistered purity. In Selma, Ralph Abernathy announced at dusk that the stymied marchers would keep vigil all night for the comatose Rev. James Reeb. . . .

The President, back in Washington from a day trip to Camp David, called Attorney General Katzenbach later Wednesday night. "This minister's gonna die, isn't he?" asked Johnson.

"Yes, sir," said Katzenbach.

"Is he already dead?" asked Johnson.

When Katzenbach said it was a matter of hours, Johnson pushed for specific actions the administration could take to meet another crescendo of unrest. Katzenbach, having apologized profusely for recommending that the President make no public statement about Bloody Sunday until a legislative proposal was ready ("Forget it," Johnson told him), presented measures that were not quite ready. That day's draft of a voting rights message was unsatisfactory. "It just doesn't sing yet," Katzenbach said. He was consulting privately with Judge Frank Johnson ("I think the judge is going to be pretty good"), but could not say so. His feverish negotiations toward a voting rights bill with Senator Everett Dirksen, who again controlled the critical Republican swing vote, had irritated Senator Mike Mansfield to the point that the Democratic Majority Leader threatened revolt over being taken for granted. "He's too polite to say that," Katzenbach reported, "but that's what he felt.". . .

[I]n a federal courtroom swamped with reporters, King testified as the first witness in Judge Frank Johnson's hearing on the proposed march to Montgomery. Lawyers for Governor Wallace and Sheriff Clark made him admit that he marched on Tuesday in spite of Judge Johnson's injunction, "even after a marshal read you the order." When they pressed him to acknowledge that he had denounced the order as "unjust," King shifted uneasily. "Yes, I did," he said. The judge interrupted the lawyers to claim the fight as his own, ruling that guilt for contempt was a matter "between this court and the alleged contemptors." Removing his glasses, he stared down from the bench to question King directly about his conversations with Governor Collins and how far he had marched beyond Pettus Bridge. Most pointedly, he asked King about a "report I have received from the Justice Department" that after the march was confronted by troopers, "they were pulled away and that their automobiles were removed while y'all were still there, is that correct?"

"That is correct," said King.

"And then did you go forward, or did you turn and go back?" asked Judge Johnson.

"We turned around and went back to Selma," said King.

"After the troopers had pulled back?"

"That is correct," said King.

"And at that point there were no troopers in front of you?"

"That is correct," said King. Heads nodded in the courtroom. The contest turned on clashing interpretations of his behavior as compliance, defiance, or shame.

Judge Johnson sternly demanded silence from spectators and admonished both sides to maintain decorum through their badgering hostilities. To circumvent his orders requiring the use of courtesy titles such as "Dr." and "Mr.," lawyers for Alabama never referred to or addressed King by name. . . .

[On Sunday, March 14,] at St. Mark's Episcopal in Washington, Rev. William Baxter preached about his own Selma journey to a congregation that included the Johnson and Humphrey families, as observances spilled widely to mark the week since Pettus Bridge. From San Jose, California, and Beloit, Wisconsin, marchers set off on fifty-mile treks to honor the impeded course from Selma to Montgomery. Twenty-seven ministers conducted a service of reconciliation at the Alamo in San Antonio, Texas, and a thousand people in New Orleans marched through hostile crowds to advocate voting rights. In Massachusetts, twenty thousand attended a "Rally for Freedom" on Boston Common, while opponents burned a ten-foot cross in the fabled revolutionary town of Lexington. A relay of eighteen freedom runners left from New York's George Washington Bridge bound for Washington, and nuns from the Sisters of Charity, in military formation and Puritan-style habits, joined a procession of 15,000 through Harlem to hear addresses by John Lewis, James Forman, and Bayard Rustin. From All Souls Unitarian Church in Washington, where James Reeb had served as assistant pastor until 1964, the morning service emptied into a spontaneous march down Sixteenth Street that gathered another crowd of 15,000 into Lafayette Park for speakers, including Fannie Lou Hamer of Mississippi. "Her plump face shining in the sun," reported the normally staid *New York Times*, "she shouted in her mighty voice: 'It's time now to stop begging them for what should have been done one hundred years ago. We have stood up on our feet, and God knows we're on our way!'"

Noise from Lafayette Park filtered across the street into the Cabinet Room where President Johnson convened seven congressional leaders Sunday afternoon. "You made the White House fireproof but not soundproof," he observed wryly in the midst of a sober prediction that more would die like Reeb until the government secured the right to register and vote for all citizens "except those in mental institutions." Senate leaders Mike Mansfield and Everett Dirksen each pressed Johnson not to seem panicky in the face of demonstrations. "This is a deliberate government," said Dirksen. "Don't let those people say, 'we scared him into it.'" Perhaps by prearrangement, House leaders argued that a presidential address to the nation would instill relief rather than panic. "I think it would help," said Majority Leader Carl Albert of Oklahoma, and Speaker John McCormack invited Johnson to address a joint session of Congress. They fixed Tuesday evening as the earliest practicable time for the President to put his proposals into speech form, but Attorney General Katzenbach allowed that the "unpredictable" King might try to resume the march from Selma earlier the same day. To preclude being upstaged, the leaders resolved to advance the date to Monday—the next evening.

King with a weary President Lyndon Johnson. The Vietnam War frayed their historic alliance.

— CHAPTER THIRTEEN —

Crossroads in Vietnam: LBJ and MLK, 1965

As expected, in his televised speech to Congress that Monday, March 15, President Johnson proposed a comprehensive bill to end voting discrimination by race. What startled the nation was his sweeping intimacy. "At times," he began, "history and fate meet at a single time in a single place to shape a turning point in man's unending search for freedom. So it was at Lexington and Concord. So it was a century ago at Appomattox. So it was last week in Selma, Alabama."

From this opening salute, which welcomed a Negro-led movement into the heart of American patriotism, Johnson advocated its cause with unflinching personal testimony. "Because it is not just Negroes, but really it's all of us," he concluded, "who must overcome the crippling legacy of bigotry and injustice—and—we—shall—overcome." Legislators gasped to hear a hard-nosed president from Texas adopt what had been the anthem of troublesome street protest. A few suspected some hidden ploy. Most soon accepted that Johnson had chosen carefully the political moment to reveal his true purpose.

By cruel coincidence, Johnson was making his fateful choice also about nascent war in Vietnam. The first U.S. combat division landed there precisely on Selma's Bloody Sunday. Johnson would always conceal his inner judgment on the war, sharply in contrast with his forthright address on voting rights. "Vietnam makes the chills run up my back," he told a mentor in secret. His security advisers foresaw no way to impose a permanent victory on foreign soil, but Johnson feared political ruin if he looked weak or accepted defeat. "I don't think anything is gonna be as bad as losing," he confided. In March, pressed for the deployment to forestall humiliation, he replied, "My judgment is no, but my answer is yes." He weighed an urgent request for another 200,000 troops four months later.

King, meanwhile, explored sites for a nonviolent movement against racial prejudice in the North—testing Boston, Rochester, Cleveland, Philadelphia, and his eventual choice, Chicago. Pressing exhausted colleagues, who were reluctant to leave their unconsolidated gains in familiar Southern territory, he insisted that a vanguard movement must confront racial prejudice beyond the sectional glare of segregation laws.

Swiftly, by summer, King and President Johnson became star-crossed allies. Pressed for public comment, King called Vietnam "a serious problem" for which violent escalation "is accomplishing nothing." Such mild dissent froze King's communications with a White House that projected sovereign control and demanded loyalty. Poignantly, King reached out to Johnson himself. Both men skirted the radioactive war topic. With the voting rights bill still hanging in the balance, they savored Selma's unique collaboration between a citizen's movement and elected government. They managed only a thin glancing truce on Vietnam.

[From *At Canaan's Edge*, pp. 252–55, 268–70]

K ing announced that morning at the Palmer House that he had agreed "to spend some time in Chicago, beginning July 24." To skeptical questions about the point of demonstrations in a city without segregation laws, he replied that many "persons of good will" did not yet understand the breadth of the nonviolent movement, and that there was "a great job of interpretation to be done" before his first major campaign in the North. "During entire press conference," FBI observers cabled headquarters, "King was not questioned nor did he mention Viet Nam, or make any reference whatsoever to United States foreign policy." Leaving Andrew Young with Bevel to prepare his Chicago canvass, King flew to New York for an afternoon engagement and promptly canceled his evening flight to Los Angeles. There were too many ominous signs radiating over telephone lines, seeping into news—and too many historic changes teetering—for him to be content with guesses about the single most crucial vector in democracy. When an incoming call rang through on July 7 at 8:05 P.M., the White House log recorded Lyndon Johnson's first phone conversation initiated by King.

The President came on the line distant and cold. He grunted without recognition until King confirmed his name: "This is Martin King."

"Yes."

"How do you do, sir?"

"Fine."

"Fine," said King. "Glad to hear your voice."

"Thank you."

Johnson's clipped monosyllables hung until King abandoned pleasantry to ask about the voting rights bill. "I want to get your advice on this," he concluded.

Deference thawed the President. "I'll be glad to," he said, cranking into political calculations of such sustained acceleration that King would speak only one word ("very") over the next ten minutes. Johnson saw the opposing coalition of Republicans and crafty Southerners becoming more potent since Goldwater began to influence Republican leaders in Congress. "They're gonna quit the nigras," he said. "They will not let a nigra vote for them." Their current ploy was "to get a big fight started over which way to repeal the poll tax," he summarized, telling King that the Senate very nearly passed an amendment to abolish poll taxes as a form of racial discrimination, but the administration detected a mousetrap. Vermont had a dormant poll tax law, and Katzenbach warned that segregationists would welcome the amendment as an opening to challenge the overall bill from a state with virtually no Negroes. "They'll bring the case on Vermont," the President told King. "And that'll be the case that they'll take to the Court, and they will not hold that it is discriminatory in Vermont because it is not." Having originally instructed Katzenbach "to get rid of the poll tax any way in the world he could without nullifying the whole law," Johnson said Katzenbach's legal strategy was good politics. He vowed to keep the bill clean, and move separately to speed one of the pending Southern cases by which the Supreme Court was expected to void all poll taxes.

Johnson complained that House liberals could not resist temptation to add a poll tax amendment anyway. "[Speaker John] McCormack was afraid that somebody would be stronger for the Negro than he was," he fumed, "so he came out red hot for complete repeal." The imminent vote could be fatal, he told King, because any slight change in the Senate-passed bill would require a conference committee of both houses of Congress to reconcile differences. "So they get in an argument, and that delays it," he said. "And maybe nothing comes out." Any modified bill must repeat the legislative process in at least one chamber of Congress, and either hurdle a filibuster again in the Senate or "you got to go back to Judge [Howard] Smith" in the House. "You got to get a rule from him, and he won't give you a rule. He, he, he," Johnson sputtered, on the pitfalls of recircumventing the implacable Rules Committee chairman from Virginia. "So you got to file a [discharge] petition and take another twenty-one days . . . and they want to get out of here Labor Day. And they're playin' for that time. Now they been doin' that for thirty-five years that I been here, and I been watchin' 'em do it."

More than once Johnson reminded King of "my practical political problem" with the two Kennedy senators, both of whom supported poll tax repeal. He portrayed himself as a lonely president embattled on a dozen fronts while his civil rights allies were "all off celebratin'"—Wilkins at his convention, labor leaders George Meany and Walter Reuther on vacation, "and you're somewhere else." The opposition was "playin' us," said Johnson, "and we are not parliamentary smart enough, if you want to be honest—now you asked advice, I'm just tellin' you." He worked up a lather of shrewdness, rage, and self-pity that tickled King in spite of himself. "They want your wife to go one direction and you to go the other," said the President.

"Yes," said King, chuckling.

"Then the kids don't know which one to follow," added Johnson.

King laughed as the President rounded through his tactical blueprint. "Well, I certainly appreciate this, Mr. President," he said, adding softly that he was confident in Katzenbach on "this whole voting bill," and that always he had tried to make the movement helpful, "as I was telling you when we started in Alabama."

"You sure have and—" said Johnson. He checked himself, then responded more earnestly to King's personal reminder. "Well, you helped, I think, to dramatize and bring it to a point where I could go before the

Congress in that night session, and I think that was one of the most effective things that ever happened," he declared. "But, uh, you had worked for months to help create the sentiment that supported it."

"Yes," said King.

"Now the trouble is that fire has gone out," added Johnson, not lingering on sentiment. "We got a few coals on it," he said, then reviewed his plan to stoke the embers with cedar and "a little coal oil" by full-scale civil rights lobby for a unified bill in the House.

"Yes, well, this has been very sound," King replied, quickly interjecting "one other point that I wanted to mention to you, because it has begun to concern me a great deal, in the last, uh, few days, in making my speeches, in making a speech in Virginia, where I made a statement concerning, uh, the Vietnam situation, and there have been some press statements about it." The President kept silent through King's nervous monologue denying that he was "engaged in destructive criticism . . . that we should unilaterally withdraw troops from Vietnam, which I know is unreasonable." He had been "speaking really as a minister of the gospel," King said, and wanted to be clear. "It was merely a statement that *all* citizens of good will ought to be concerned about the problem that faces our world, the problem of war," he added carefully, "and that, although uncomfortable, they ought to debate on this issue." King coughed. "I just wanted to say that *to* you," he said, "because I felt eventually that it would come to your attention—"

"Well—"

"—and I know the terrible burden and awesome responsibility and decisions that you make, and I know it's complicated," King rushed on, "and I didn't want to add to the burdens because I know they're very difficult."

Johnson paused. "Well, you, you, you're very, uh, uh, helpful, and I appreciate it," he said, stumbling. Then he recovered: "I *did* see it. I *was* distressed. I *do* want to talk to you." He exposed to King his confessional tone about Vietnam, saying he had stalled and hoped to the point that "unless I bomb, they run me out right quick," and stressed the constant toll of war pressure—"well, the Republican leader had a press conference this afternoon, [Gerald] Ford, demanded I bomb Hanoi"—over his twenty months in office. "I've lost about two hundred and sixty—our lives up to now," he told King, "and I could lose two hundred and sixty-five *thousand* mighty easy, and I'm trying to keep those zeroes down."

The President admitted that he was "not all wise" in matters of foreign policy. "I don't want to be a warmonger," he assured King, but neither could he abide defeat in a Cold War conflict. "Now I don't want to pull down the flag and come home runnin' with my tail between my legs," he said, "particularly if it's going to create more problems than I got out there—and it *would,* according to our best judges." Johnson urged King to explore the alternatives at length with Secretary of State Dean Rusk, Defense Secretary Robert McNamara, and himself—"I'll give you all I know"—and thanked him for constructive purpose always "in our dealings together." King in turn thanked Johnson for true leadership, and especially—"I don't think I've had a chance"—for his speech after Selma. They parted with pledges of joint zeal to finish the quest for universal suffrage.

At their fleeting, crucial moment of contact on Vietnam, Johnson had minimized his war motive to the point of apology, just as King circumscribed his criticism. Each one said he yearned to find another way, but shied from nonviolent strategies in the glare of the military challenge. . . .

On Wednesday, July 28, the President ordered his staff to rustle up cushioning news to surround the Vietnam announcement at noon. Twelve minutes beforehand, Johnson himself called his trusted legal adviser Abe Fortas. "How is your blood pressure?" he asked coyly. . . .

Surveys recorded a daytime television audience of 28 million, with only 4 percent of sets tuned elsewhere. "Once the Communists know, as we know that a violence solution is impossible," said Johnson, "then a peaceful solution is inevitable." Reporters noted that Lady Bird Johnson covered her face, near tears, as he reprised from his Selma speech. . . . Defying undertow, President Johnson rose buoyantly to other matters. He introduced his nominee to head the Voice of America, NBC News correspondent John Chancellor . . . and presented as a startling surprise, even to himself, the soon-to-be appointed Supreme Court Justice Fortas. . . .

Thursday's *New York Times* spread war news across three giant tiers, "JOHNSON ORDERS 50,000 MORE MEN / TO VIETNAM AND DOUBLES DRAFT / AGAIN URGES U.N. TO SEEK PEACE." Surrounding front-page stories headlined restraint—"Most in Congress Relieved," said one, alongside "Economic Impact Is Called Slight." The *Times* editorial rested on his "vital" point that the war must be "held down to the absolute minimum necessary to prove to Hanoi and Peking that military aggression is not worthwhile," and the principal news dispatch, "NO RESERVE CALL," recognized that the President avoided congressional scrutiny of a disruptive, costly deployment by declining to activate Reserve forces. He called instead for an extra 18,000 draftees per month.

Draftees would supply politically convenient soldiers only for the moment, as Johnson well knew, but his overriding worry was that candid mobilization would touch off hawkish alarms for unfettered war. "Don't pay any attention to what the little shits on the campuses do," he told the Undersecretary of State, George Ball. "The great beast is the reactionary elements in this country." At the same time, Johnson railed that realistic disclosures would backfire to the aid of dovish critics in Congress. Public exchanges "just put water on Mansfield's and on Morse's paddle," he fretted to Eisenhower, longing for acquiescence on all sides. "If we could get Morse *and* Ford to quit talking," he opined, "it would be a lot better." To minimize debate, and the need for concurrence, he assumed the burden of war on his own claim of authority. An elastic conscription law allowed him to commandeer manpower for Vietnam by quiet executive decree, at the price of inevitable protest that no such autocratic power should compel young Americans to kill or be killed in the name of free government.

During one of King's marches for integrated housing in Chicago's all-white neighborhoods, young people attack isolated demonstrators arriving by car.

— CHAPTER FOURTEEN —

Nonviolence Goes North: King in Chicago, 1966

The national argument about race shifted north just before King launched his movement in Chicago. That argument was blurry and new, seeking adaptation or relief in a period of rapid historical change. More landmarks won approval into permanent national law through the second half of 1965. In July came the Medicare Act to provide health care for senior citizens. In August, overcoming another determined Southern filibuster, Congress passed a Voting Rights Act that would enfranchise three million previously excluded minority voters. In October, the Immigration Reform Act of 1965 repealed a system that had confined most legal immigration to applicants from the white nations of Northern Europe. "Never again," Johnson vowed at a signing ceremony beneath the Statue of Liberty, would the race-based quota system "shadow the gate to the American nation with the twin barriers of prejudice and privilege."

A seminal riot interrupted the legislative streak. In August, four days of upheaval devastated the Watts neighborhood of Los Angeles—killing 35 people and injuring 1,032, nearly 90 percent Negroes. The *Los Angeles Times* hired its first Negro reporter to penetrate the sealed-off riot areas. Shocked observers, wondering what grievances there could be in sunny California, debated whether a sinister conspiracy or "insensate rage" had precipitated the violence. The Los Angeles police chief proclaimed victory: "We're on top, and they're on the bottom." The Los Angeles mayor rejected calls to investigate tribal attitudes in his police department, saying, "Race relations would go to a low ebb, because the white community would not stand for it."

Reporters asked King to interpret the Watts riot in light of a sensational new report by Daniel Patrick Moynihan, a sociology professor working for the U.S. Labor Department. Moynihan postulated that the Negro family in general was infected by a "tangle of pathology," indicated chiefly by a high rate of female-headed families and a corresponding low self-esteem in Negro men. "The very essence of the male animal, from the bantam rooster to the four-star general, is to strut," he wrote. ". . . Not for the Negro male. The 'sassy nigger' was lynched." Moynihan's thesis touched off warring new interpretations over gender, reverse racism, and the objectivity of white experts.

In November, a literary rebirth pitched into the storm of reaction. The *New York Times*, which had scorned Malcolm X at his death in February for "a pitifully wasted life" and "a ruthless and fanatical belief in violence," hailed his "brilliant, painful, important book." *Time* magazine would classify the posthumous *Autobiography of Malcolm X* among the ten best nonfiction books of the twentieth century. "I know nothing of the South," wrote Malcolm. "I am the creation of the northern white man and of his hypocritical attitude toward the Negro." His flinty realism suited a national climate that was hardening over war and dissent.

[From *At Canaan's Edge*, pp. 374–76, 407–8, 427–28, 440–44]

Like the Moynihan report, which omitted policy recommendations to concentrate on its thesis of family pathology, the *Autobiography* disregarded goals and ideas for reform. "It tells what happens to an intelligent Negro who discovers that he has, within American society, no future," observed the *Times* review. "And it tells in the most powerful and precise terms what this really means—the systematized destruction of Negro self-esteem as an almost automatic function of white society." Malcolm scorched the promise of American democracy. "I am not interested in becoming American," he said, "because America is not interested in me."...

No one could have foreseen that the year of the Voting Rights Act would conclude in lasting effusions over "Negro matriarchy" and Malcolm X. Both aimed to penetrate the broken heart of race without suggesting salves or remedies. Both discarded in passing the nonviolent methods of the civil rights movement. One mingled the wobbliest and sharpest tools of social science to redefine the issue on a presumption that Americans "have gone beyond equal opportunity." The other insisted flatly from the grave that race scarcely had budged, and that the benevolent white liberal was a fraud. "I don't care how nice one is to you," wrote Malcolm X, ". . . almost never does he see you as he sees himself, as he sees his own kind."

Split images hovered over a changing landscape. Even sports remained white at Southern colleges until a lone basketball player made the Maryland roster in November. The first two Negro high school students were signing scholarships for Southeastern Conference football at Kentucky, though neither would ever play a game. (One quit after the other died of a broken back suffered in practice, which obliged the university to resolve suspicions of violent discrimination by teammates.) Shortsighted experts debated which Negroes and colleges might dare to step forward, while professional teams rushed ahead into newly integrated markets. By December, hastening to Atlanta behind the [Major League Baseball] Milwaukee Braves, a new football franchise presold its 1966 tickets before receiving any players or even choosing its Falcons nickname. Comedian Danny Thomas helped organize a team called the Miami Dolphins. . . .

Observers noticed a fundamental shift in attitude toward urban areas. "No other nation hates its own cities," wrote columnist TRB for *The New Republic*. "Only in the USA are suburbs afraid of their parents." The editors of *Life* magazine prepared for December a double issue called "The U.S. City." Half the spreads displayed dazzling lights, sophisticated people, and futuristic designs with matching headlines—"The Proud Shapes," "Trains That Need No Wheels," "Satellites, Megastructures, Platforms," "Homework Done by Computer." The other half showcased grim tenements and hungry children—"A Bitter and Insistent Plague," "Racial Trap," "Torn Family." Scholar Herbert Gans observed more than a decade later that the *Life* issue marked an abrupt end to media celebrations of urban vitality, which traditionally overlooked or romanticized desperado street wars among the poor. Connotations of the word "city," whose Greek root supplied the ancient concept and name for politics itself, sagged under impressions suffused with race. . . .

On Friday [January 7, 1966] in Chicago, at what the *New York Times* called "a crowded news conference in the garish red-and-gold Gigi Room of the plush Sahara Motel," Martin Luther King released a thirteen-page launch blueprint for "the first significant Northern freedom movement." For the betterment of greater Chicago, whose Negroes had come to out-number those in all Mississippi, he announced a new campaign aimed at conditions broader than de facto school segregation or the harsh legacy of the rural South. "This economic exploitation is crystallized in the SLUM," said King, which he defined as "an area where free trade and exchange of culture and resources is not allowed to exist . . . a system of internal colonialism not unlike the exploitation of the Congo by Belgium." His Chicago blueprint identified trade unions and welfare boards among twelve institutions that perpetuated slums in an interlocking pattern difficult to understand, he acknowledged, let alone to change. (Five unions shut down final construction on the monumental Gateway Arch project that same day in St. Louis, because a contractor had hired the first Negro plumber under sustained pressure from the new U.S. Office of Federal Contract Compliance.)

King announced an escalating series of community rallies, organizing drives, and test demonstrations to culminate in May, but he hedged predictions by analogy with the voting rights campaign launched a year earlier. "Just as no one knew on January 2, 1965, that there would be a march from Selma to Montgomery," he announced, "so now we are in no position to know what form massive action might take in Chicago." The uncertainty of future confrontation muted news coverage, but King gained banner headlines in the *Defender* with a promise to move his own family into a freezing local tenement before the end of January: "Dr. King Will Occupy Chicago Slum Flat in New Rights Drive / He's Out to Close Ghetto.". . .

King began weekly slum residence that Wednesday afternoon [January 26]. From the Chicago airport, he was whisked secretly to mediate the lingering frictions over his proposed location. A few leaders from the city-wide civil rights coalition considered it belittling to their hopes that a renowned international figure would advertise black Chicago's most extreme degradation. Some argued that there were plenty of distinguished homes and hovels alike in historic South Side "Bronzeville." Others objected that James Bevel had ignored neighborhood partners in an awkward search for the most symbolic site on the lowly West Side. Word surfaced that traveling

aide Bernard Lee had pronounced eight vacancies "unlivable," and landlords recoiled from King's name on the lease, so Lee was obliged to conceal
the intended occupant by signing himself. Newspapers discovered the ruse.
Their emphasis on last-minute refurbishment by the panicked landlord—
"King Picks 'Typical' Flat/8 Men Repair It," reported the *Chicago Tribune*—
projected an air of fiasco and false humility for the Chicago campaign.

King appraised the sniping as normal. "I can learn more about the
situation by being here with those who live and suffer here," he insisted,
then proceeded by caravan into the West Side ghetto of North Lawndale,
nicknamed "Slumdale" by residents. A crowd of several hundred waited
numbly in the cold to observe the entourage enter a third-floor walk-up
at 1550 South Hamlin Avenue. Coretta, looking ahead to the small comfort of promised improvements upstairs, stepped first into the shock of a
lockless ground-floor entry with a bare dirt floor. "The smell of urine was
overpowering," she recalled. "We were told that this was because the door
was always open, and drunks came in off the street to use the hallway as
a toilet." Above, fresh coats of gray and yellow paint did cover the empty
apartment of four narrow rooms and "a bath of sorts," lined single-file from
the street to overlook a back alley. "You had to go through the bedrooms
to get to the kitchen," Coretta noted. They broke away from unpacking for
King to deliver an evening speech at Chicago Theological Seminary, where
new SCLC staff member Jesse Jackson was a student, then returned to a
steady stream of first-night neighbors, including children who darted in to
gawk. Bob Black of the *Chicago Defender* photographed eight-year-old Roy
Williams sitting shyly on King's lap. Six curious members of the local Vice
Lords gang stayed late in discussion with King about their turf battles and
his concept of nonviolence.

As he first walked the streets to sample Lawndale and nearby East
Garfield, trailing reporters noticed faces peering at the phenomenon from
open windows even in zero-degree weather. One old man nearly collapsed
when he recognized the famous preacher, and mumbled, "Great God
a'mighty, I didn't ever think this day would come." Many in the path remained skeptical about change, however, saying the black people who had

made it to Chicago were divided and reluctant to risk what little they had. "It's bad enough to be at the top of nothing," said one mother, "but to be at the *bottom* of nothing?" On Thursday, Chicago's protest leader Al Raby guided King from a bustling soul food lunch at Belinda's Pit to a courtesy tour of police headquarters. Press interest fluttered to every hint of future conflict, as when King assured Chief Orlando Wilson that he would give ample notice before marches or civil disobedience. Wilson tried to be gracious by confirming his surprise discovery of some Irish ancestry in King (pretty far back, on Daddy King's side), which he said never hurt in shamrock Chicago. . . .

After changing into work clothes that afternoon at his Hamlin Avenue apartment, King led a procession of two hundred people through bitter cold to a six-unit tenement house, where he announced from the steps that the Chicago Freedom Movement was assuming "trusteeship" on behalf of tenants who had begged for help. He said the building had no heat, was unfit for habitation, and the $400 per month aggregate rent would be appropriated for vital repairs. King invoked "supralegal" authority. "The moral question is far more important than the legal one," he said, then trooped inside with a work party to clean ashes from the furnace. Changing clothes again, he addressed a Wednesday night education rally at Jenner School before keeping a late engagement at the South Chicago home of Elijah Muhammad. The Nation of Islam leader had sought an introduction through intermediaries for years, never harder than now, across awkward gaps of custom and public dispute. Coretta was asked to sit separately with the Muslim women. King and Muhammad found chatting ground as fellow preacher's kids from Georgia, the former Elijah Poole having grown up a "whooping" Baptist in his native Cordele. King readily agreed that he found the struggle of nonviolence "not always easy," but he could not coax from Muhammad even a wink of pulpit guile about his sectarian doctrine that all white people were created devils. The old man rigidly scolded Al Raby for having married a white woman, and smiled only when King said he doubted they could reach a productive understanding. "All we have to do is drink a cup of coffee," Muhammad responded. That week, for their annual Savior's Day Convention, Nation of Islam house organs trumpeted the King summit as another symbolic wonder from the one they venerated as Holy Apostle of Islam.

Public attention fastened upon a clash of race and real estate, leaving the Muslim audience only squib notice outside the Negro press. "Dr. King Seizes a Slum Building," announced the February 24 *New York Times,* which covered the escalating conflict the next day: "Dr. King Assailed for Slum Tactic." From New York, Stanley Levison called on his wiretapped phone line to criticize the surrender of the legal high ground in Chicago, but Andrew Young said they could not afford the numb delay of a lawsuit. Unforgettably, he had seen a shivering baby wrapped in newspapers. "We *wanted* to do it illegally," he told Levison. "We want to be put in jail for furnishing heat and health requirements to people with children in the winter." Levison approved of his courage but not the result. A prominent black federal judge denounced the takeover as theft. Mayor Richard Daley, while reprimanding the use of "illegal ways" to improve slums, refused to prosecute or jail King and then charged the landlord with code violations, while announcing a crash city program to inspect 15,000 buildings on the West Side. The slum owner turned out to be an eighty-one-year-old invalid instead of a sleek profiteer. "I think King is right," John Bender told reporters, offering his property to anyone who would assume the mortgage.

Staff effort salvaged a remarkable mass meeting at which two owners of more substantial slum investment faced grievances under King's protection, flanking him on the platform of the movement's citywide headquarters, Warren Avenue Congregational in East Garfield. One by one, tenants came forward hesitantly with church-style "testimony" about rats and rotted floors. "Don't be afraid," the evening's pulpit mistress cajoled. "Your *landlord* wasn't afraid to come here." John Condor, given the chance to respond, introduced himself and partner Lou Costalis as residents of the neighborhood before and since the massive white flight of the 1950s. "We're with you, believe it or not," he announced.

"No, you ain't!" shouted a voice. Occasional catcalls escaped a generally hushed crowd as the white landlords pleaded helplessness, arguing that "the big boys" in the downtown business Loop constricted slums with "red-line" bank restrictions to favor concentrated public housing and marginal ghetto business over home ownership. "Don't fight the wrong fight," pleaded Condor.

King closed with thanks to the landlords for putting a human face on complex injustice, then lifted the crowd from a queasy, anticlimactic mood by preaching on familiar themes. "We are somebody because we are God's children," cried King. ("That's right!" answered voices from the pews.) "You don't need to hate anybody," he said—violence would only meet greater force, but nonviolence could march into the hearts of opponents and bystanders alike. He exhorted them to organize by door-to-door canvass across Chicago. "We are going to change the whole Jericho road!" shouted King, and the landlords themselves joined in the applause. . . .

Stanley Levison urgently recommended program cutbacks in either Chicago or the South to reduce SCLC's burgeoning debt, but grumbled that King "mopped the floor" with his unwelcome advice at an emergency conference in Atlanta, resolving instead to intensify fund-raising between weekly circuits into Chicago. . . . The next night, Saturday, March 12, Harry Belafonte welcomed a sellout crowd of 12,000 to the Freedom Festival benefit at the Chicago International Amphitheater, where King described Chicago as the giant of migrant black communities stretching from Watts and Blackbottom Detroit to Harlem and Roxbury Boston. Northern ghettos had locked down bodies and hopes "even unto the third and fourth generation," he said, and the sixty thousand chronically unemployed Negroes of Chicago would be called "a staggering depression" in white society. With a voice that conveyed anguished hope like fire from a well-sealed wood stove, he exhorted his audience to "plunge deeper into the philosophy of nonviolence" as they fought to spread the "new democracy" bursting from the South.

"Never before in the history of the civil rights movement," King declared from the Chicago stage, "has an action campaign been launched in such splendor." The event netted $80,000. Stanley Levison called home to pronounce his weekend visit "terribly exciting" in spite of prior misgivings about a Northern campaign: "You could see that this was an audience with spirit, a fighting audience." He said King had to hide from a crush of visitors to his slum apartment. "When they start mass action in the spring," Levison predicted, "that is when everyone will start paying attention."

SNCC Chair Stokely Carmichael drew crowds nationwide after he proclaimed a new "black power" slogan in Mississippi.

CHAPTER FIFTEEN

Black Power, 1966

Stokely Carmichael, a charismatic young SNCC veteran from Trinidad and New York, suffered a brief nervous breakdown before the final march out of Selma in 1965. On recovery, he conceived an alternative to the enervating strife among SNCC rivals overshadowed by Martin Luther King. Instead of what he called "ignore King" (Silas Norman), "be King" (John Lewis), "fight King" (James Forman), or "cooperate selectively with King" (Ivanhoe Donaldson), Carmichael resolved to "use King," meaning to embrace, harness, and redirect King's popularity among the common people.

Accordingly, Carmichael trailed among the marchers toward Montgomery, introducing himself as King's disciple to curious inhabitants, and stayed on afterward in Lowndes County's nearly medieval peonage for Negroes. Ku Klux Klan bushwhackers killed a white northern volunteer, Viola Liuzzo, on a highway there the night King's march ended. Three of Carmichael's movement friends were shot in the next few months, including Episcopal seminarian Jonathan Daniels and Tuskegee student Sammy Younge. Of these only Richard Morrisroe, a novice Catholic priest from Chicago, would survive his grave wounds. Sometimes Carmichael awkwardly rode a mule to canvass the isolated sharecropper cabins. His tiny SNCC project at first celebrated each local resident who dared to register for the vote. By January of 1966, a crude "Tent City" housed those evicted for trying.

Nevertheless, nearly a thousand members of the Lowndes County Freedom Organization became qualified voters for the May 1966 Alabama primary. They decided also to nominate a slate of candidates for local offices such as sheriff and county clerk. Because state law required ballots to identify each party with a visual symbol, which for Alabama Democrats was the rooster of white supremacy, the fledgling party adopted a black panther traced from the mascot of a college football team. Outdoors, under tense federal protection, members of the original "Black Panther" party cast the first real ballots of their lives. Most were elderly farm people.

All this escaped public notice. Although the new party's nominees could not yet win election in remote Lowndes County, where the small white minority ruled tightly by fiat, Carmichael did gain credit within movement circles for a stupendous feat of grassroots mobilization under primitive conditions. His SNCC peers ousted John Lewis to elect him national chair only days after the primary. Weary of nonviolence, Carmichael soon seized a national spotlight for SNCC.

On June 6, a shotgun ambush wounded the integration pioneer

James Meredith on his lone "March Against Fear." Carmichael joined national civil rights leaders in a spontaneous vow to complete Meredith's intended route through Mississippi—some 230 miles, more than four times the march from Selma to Montgomery. Reporters and intrepid volunteers swelled the ranks from afar. Approaching Greenwood, Martin Luther King broke away briefly to tend his movement in Chicago.

[From *At Canaan's Edge*, pp. 485–95]

Carmichael cross-examined colleagues nightly about their field tests of a new SNCC slogan, still doubting he could count on the response [Willie] Ricks claimed for crowd-building speeches in familiar cotton fields and churches ahead. Greenwood had been a movement foothold since Bob Moses dared to enter the Delta in 1962. Carmichael himself had lived and gone to jail there as regional director for the 1964 Freedom Summer project. He knew the police chief, "Buff" Hammond, as a relative moderate, but their schoolyard encounter swiftly deteriorated on Thursday afternoon, June 16. Carmichael said police must be blocking the advance tent crews by mistake, as weary marchers had to camp at the only public space available to Negroes; Hammond said any assembly on the grounds of Stone Street Negro School required a permit from the all-white school board, which was closed. "We'll put them up anyway," Carmichael protested. Officers handcuffed him and two others.

A historical moment teetered for six hours. By supper, King issued a statement from Chicago on the Mississippi crackdown. FBI wiretappers forwarded from New York to Washington Stanley Levison's judgment that political pressure was hardening Governor Paul Johnson, along with King's comment that he "had expected something like this" because "the police were too polite" and the march "just did not feel like Mississippi." In Greenwood, where the morning *Commonwealth* warned against King as a hatemonger "who can be compared to Josef Stalin and Mao Tze Tung," local officials thought better of dispersing his hordes. They reversed themselves to allow the school campsite, which added jolts of vindication to the mass meeting that night. Willie Ricks guided Carmichael to the speaker's platform when he made bail, saying most of the locals remembered him fondly. "Drop it now!" he urged. "The people are ready."

Carmichael faced an agitated crowd of six hundred. "This is the 27th time I have been arrested," he began, "and I ain't going to jail no more!" He said Negroes should stay home from Vietnam and fight for black power in Greenwood. "We want black power!" he shouted five times, jabbing his forefinger downward in the air. "That's right. That's what we want, black power. We don't have to be ashamed of it. We have stayed here. We have begged the president. We've begged the federal government—that's all we've been doing, begging and begging. It's time we stand up and take over. Every courthouse in Mississippi ought to be burned down tomorrow to get rid of the dirt and the mess. From now on, when they ask you what you want, you know what to tell 'em. What do you want?"

The crowd shouted, "Black power!" Willie Ricks sprang up to help lead thunderous rounds of call and response: "What do you want?" "Black power!"

King returned to a movement flickering starkly in its public face. At the mass meeting on Friday, June 17, after a tense march to the Leflore County courthouse, Willie Ricks dueled King's blustery assistant Hosea Williams in alternate chants of "Black Power!" versus "Freedom!" On Saturday's march past the tiny hamlet of Itta Bena—James Bevel's hometown, three years after sharecroppers there had braved their first civil rights ceremony to mourn the assassination of Medgar Evers, only to be hauled from church by way of Greenwood jail to Parchman Penitentiary, where some were suspended by handcuffs from cell bars in the death house—King and Carmichael faced persistent interviews in motion down Highway 7 toward

Belzoni. "What do you mean," asked a broadcast reporter, "when you shout 'black power' to these people back here?"

"I mean," Carmichael replied, "that the only way that black people in Mississippi will create an attitude where they will not be shot down like pigs, where they will not be shot down like dogs, is when they get the power where they constitute a majority in counties to institute justice."

"I feel, however," King interjected, "that while believing firmly that power is necessary, that it would be difficult for me to use the phrase 'black power' because of the connotative meaning that it has for many people." Carmichael walked alongside, hands clasped behind his back with beguiling pleasantry. Both wore sunglasses. . . .

On Tuesday, June 21, King and Ralph Abernathy detoured by car with twenty volunteers from the main column to commemorate three victims of Klan murder exactly two years earlier, on the first night of Freedom Summer. Several hundred local people joined a rattled walk from Mt. Nebo Baptist Church to the Neshoba County courthouse in Philadelphia, Mississippi. Shocked employers along the sidewalk pointed out their family maids. ("Yes, it's me," the matronly Mary Batts called out to acknowledge a stare, "and I've kept your children.") Hostile drivers buzzed the lines at high speed, and one young woman shouted from the back seat of a blue convertible that swerved to a stop: "I wouldn't dirty my goddamned car with you black bastards!" When a line of officers blocked access to the courthouse lawn, Deputy Sheriff Cecil Price, face-to-face with King, granted respite for public prayer among the bystanders closing in from both sides of the narrow street, scores of them armed with pistols, clubs, and at least one garden hoe.

King turned to raise his voice above the lines kneeling back along the pavement. "In this county, Andrew Goodman, James Chaney, and Mickey Schwerner were brutally murdered," he cried. "I believe in my heart that the murderers are somewhere around me at this moment." Reporters heard "right behind you" and "you're damn right" among grunts and chuckles in response. One wrote, "King appeared to be shaken." King knew Deputy Price himself was among eighteen defendants in the pending federal conspiracy indictment, which had been filed in the absence of a state response to the murders and remained stalled in pretrial legal maneuvers.

"They ought to search their hearts," he continued out loud. "I want them to know that we are not afraid. If they kill three of us, they will have to kill all of us. I am not afraid of any man, whether he is in Michigan or Mississippi, whether he is in Birmingham or Boston." Jeers soon drowned out the closing chorus of "We Shall Overcome." Only darting blows struck the return march until someone toppled newsmen carrying heavy network cameras. "Some 25 white men surged over the television men, swinging, and then flailed into the line of march, their eyes wide with anger," observed New York Times correspondent Roy Reed. "The Negroes screamed." Attackers "hurled stones, bottles, clubs, firecrackers and shouts of obscenity," he added, and police did not intervene "until half a dozen Negroes began to fight back." That night, careening automobile posses sprayed Philadelphia's black neighborhood with gunfire. Riders in the fourth wave narrowly missed a startled FBI agent posted near the mass meeting at Mt. Nebo. Return shots from one targeted house wounded a passing vigilante, and this noisy postlude attracted a misleading headline for Reed's dramatic front-page account of the courthouse standoff: "Whites and Negroes Trade Shots."

The Philadelphia trauma intensified conflict within the movement over strategy. King, lamenting "a complete breakdown of law and order," requested federal protection in a telegram to President Johnson, and rejoined the main march in Yazoo City during a fierce debate that erupted during the Tuesday night mass meeting. Ernest Thomas of the Louisiana Deacons for Defense and Justice ridiculed hope for safety in the hands of federal agents he said were always "smiling, writing a lot of papers, sending it back to Washington, D.C." He advocated vigilante committees to meet lawless repression. "If I must die, then I have to die the way that I feel," Thomas shouted to a chorus of cheers.

King came on late with an impassioned rebuttal. "Somebody said tonight that we are in a majority," he said. "Don't fool yourself. We are not a majority in a single state. . . . We are ten percent of the population of this nation, and it would be foolish of me to stand up and tell you we are going to get our freedom by ourselves." He challenged boasts of armed promise in the isolated black-majority counties: "Who runs the National Guard of

Mississippi? How many Negroes do you have in it? Who runs the State Patrol of Mississippi?" Any vigilante campaign would backfire "the minute we started," he argued, not only in military result but also in public opinion— "And I tell you, nothing would please our oppressors more"—so that "it is impractical even to think about it." King won back the crowd with a sermon against violence. "I am not going to allow anybody to pull me so low as to use the very methods that perpetuated evil throughout our civilization," he said. "I'm sick and tired of violence. I'm tired of the war in Vietnam. I'm tired of war and conflict in the world. I'm tired of shooting. I'm tired of hatred. I'm tired of selfishness. I'm tired of evil. I'm not going to use violence no matter who says it!" Then he retired to internal debates through the night and most of Wednesday. Carmichael rejected "black equality" as an alternative to black power, insisting there was nothing inherently violent in the word "power." King vowed to leave the march if the inflammatory rhetoric continued. The leaders compromised on a pledge to avoid the overtly competitive sloganeering, which advertised divisions at the core of a small movement based within an impoverished racial minority.

President Johnson deflected King's request for federal protection by relaying assurances from Governor Paul Johnson "that all necessary protection can and will be provided." Additional units of the Mississippi Highway Patrol "were promptly dispatched," he advised from Washington, urging King to "maintain the closest liaison with Assistant Attorney General John Doar, who will remain in Mississippi until the end of the march." Johnson's reply telegram reached King late June 23 on a long day's walk through rainstorms into Canton. Latecomers were building numbers toward the finale set for Jackson, twenty miles ahead, and local supporters swelled the crowd above two thousand for a night rally on the grounds of McNeal Elementary School for Negroes, where Hosea Williams was arrested in a new dispute over permits. As tent workers rushed to put up shelter, a Highway Patrol commander announced over a megaphone: "You will not be allowed to erect the tents. If you do, you will be removed."

Hushed disbelief spread with the realization that the Highway Patrol phalanx was turning inward. "I don't know what they plan for us," King called out from the back of a flatbed truck, "but we aren't going to fight any state troopers." Giving the microphone to Carmichael, he ran his right hand nervously over his head as armed officers spread along the perimeter. Carmichael chopped the air again with his finger. "The time for running has come to an end!" he shouted, soaked in perspiration, his eyes and teeth gleaming against the dark night. "You tell them white folks in Mississippi that all the scared niggers are dead!" Cheers covered an interlude just long enough for newsmen to count sixty-one helmeted officers fastening gas masks in unison. John Doar helplessly parried a cry for intervention: "What can I do? Neither side will give an inch."

When the first loud pops sounded, King called out above the squeals that it was tear gas. "Nobody leave," he shouted. "Nobody fight back. We're going to stand our ground." The speakers' truck disappeared beneath thick white clouds, however, as guttural screams drowned out his attempt to sing "We Shall Overcome." Choking, vomiting people ran blindly or dived to the muddy ground where fumes were thinner, but charging officers kicked and clubbed them to flight with the stocks of the tear gas guns. Within half an hour, the Highway Patrol units impounded the tents and dragged from the cleared field a dozen unconscious stragglers. They revived a three-year-old boy from Toronto, Canada. Hysteria lingered in the haze. Observers called the violence "worse than Selma," and Episcopal priest Robert Castle of New Jersey wondered out loud "if democracy in Mississippi and perhaps in the United States was dead." Two friends held up Carmichael, who had collapsed and kept repeating incoherently, "They're gonna shoot again!" Andrew Young, having leapt from the speakers' truck in panic, bent at the waist to stagger through the streets, shouting hoarsely: "We're going to the *church!* We gotta worry about the *people* now!" Reporters followed King as he retreated, wiping his eyes. "In light of this, Dr. King," asked CBS News correspondent John Hart, "have you rethought any of the philosophy of nonviolence?"

"Oh, not at all," King replied. "I still feel that we've got to be nonviolent. How could we be violent in the midst of a police force like that?" To the battered remnant that night in a rendezvous church, his remarks brushed with bitterness over the "ironic" assurances received only hours before from President Johnson. "And the very same men that tear gassed us tonight," said King, "are the men that we are told will be our protectors." Catching himself, he veered into a strangely subdued reverie: "You know, the one thing I have learned . . . on this march is that it is a shame before almighty God that people earn as little money as the Negro people of Mississippi. You know the story." He spoke of the humbling, bonding effect of seeing faces in desperation so closely. . . .

In private, King conceded to his advisers that the Meredith march had been a "terrible mistake," but he insisted that its troubles lay beyond the publicized internal squabbles. While he tolerated the loyal exuberance of subalterns like Hosea Williams, who contested SNCC rivals in everything from card games and water pistol ambushes to shoving matches, King respected SNCC's earned right to an independent voice. "Listen, Andy," he told Young, "if Stokely is saying the same thing I am saying, he becomes like my assistant." He teased Willie Ricks over his new nickname, "Black Power," in a way that Ricks prized as collegial recognition from a lifelong master of striking fire in an audience. When King said he lacked only clothes to make a fine minister, Ricks boldly asked to borrow some, and King surprised him with an invitation to take freely from his closet in Atlanta. When Carmichael confessed that he had used King's fame as a platform to test the black power slogan, King shrugged, "I have been used before." For all their strategic arguments, which outsiders fanned into a presumption of deep enmity, King and Carmichael discovered a common sense of fun to relieve tedium and tension on the exposed hike through Mississippi. On the last night, King bolted from interminable disputes about overdue bills and the rally program. "I'm sorry, y'all," he told the collected leadership. "James Brown is on. I'm gone." Carmichael hurried with King from a dean's house to musical bedlam on the Tougaloo College football field, where the soul star Brown writhed in French cuffs and a pompadour through a freedom concert arranged by Harry Belafonte. . . .

A *New York Times* retrospective said the Meredith march "made it clear that a new philosophy is sweeping the civil rights movement. . . . It had Mr. Carmichael as its leader and the late Malcolm X as its prophet. It also had a battle cry, 'Black Power,' and a slogan directed at whites, 'Move on Over, or We'll Move on Over YOU.' . . . Reporters and cameramen drawn to a demonstration by the magic of Dr. King's name stay to write about and photograph Mr. Carmichael." Primal signals compelled action in distant quarters. Within a month, religious thinkers bought space in the *Times* to interpret "the crisis brought upon our country by historic distortions of important human realities." Their joint composition—"BLACK POWER: Statement by National Committee of Negro Churchmen"—rode the conceptual mix of theology and blackness like a fresh rodeo bull, using the noun "power" fifty-five times. "We are faced now with a situation where conscience-less power meets powerless conscience," declared the consortium of bishops and pastors, "threatening the very foundation of our nation."

Stanley Levison downgraded the contagion with a jeweler's eye for politics. To him, the cry of black power disguised a lack of broad support for SNCC and CORE with cultural fireworks that amounted to an extravagant death rattle. "They're just going to die of attrition," he predicted when King called after midnight on July 1, "and as they die they're going to be noisier and more militant in their expression. . . . Because they're weak, they're making a lot of noise, and we don't want to fall into that trap." Levison, perceiving a larger obstacle than the demise of two civil rights groups, worried that the movement's historic achievements were not consolidated enough to resist or reverse what King called a "mood of violence" throughout the country. He deflected King's instinctive response to formulate a warning about the spillover dangers of "defensive violence," an understandable and prevalent doctrine. When King pressed to "clarify many misconceptions" and to refine nonviolence as "a social strategy for change" in the democratic tradition, Levison gently but firmly said he and literary agent Joan Daves had unearthed no interest. New York publishers and magazine editors considered King's position "well-known and obvious." They wanted something novel and strong. Black power was hot, whether or not it would last. King was too Sunday School, and he no longer commanded attention at the White House.

April 4, 1967, in New York's Riverside Church: King denounces the Vietnam War exactly one year before his death, flanked by seminary president John Bennett, historian Henry Steele Commager, and Rabbi Abraham Heschel (*left to right*).

CHAPTER SIXTEEN

Race and War: King at the Riverside Church, 1967

James Bevel tweaked Chicago's Democratic boss, Mayor Richard Daley, by vowing to lead demonstrations from the ghetto into the city's segregated neighborhoods "until every white person out there joins the Republican Party." King himself recruited black gang lords to accept nonviolent discipline, marching with an interracial mix of clergy and citizens to challenge real estate practices that confined and exploited black residents. In August of 1966, they met howling white mobs that felled King with stones. "I have never in my life seen such hate," he said. "Not in Mississippi or Alabama. This is a terrible thing."

The Chicago movement finally negotiated a settlement with Daley and the city's top banks, Realtors, and churches, including the Catholic Archdiocese. Its modest terms were stronger than previous local outcomes in Birmingham or Selma, but there was no corresponding national surge. Instead, a sharp political backlash countered the tides of 1963 and 1965. Georgia elected a novice governor, restaurant owner Lester Maddox, who was known for defying the new civil rights law by chasing away black customers at gunpoint. Maddox denied any racial animus or appeal, as did Ronald Reagan, who won the California governorship after opposing both major civil rights acts in 1964 and 1965. President Johnson suffered heavy reversals in the congressional midterms. "I think the Negroes lost it," he groaned privately, fretting that the backlash would "move beyond George Wallace and become respectable."

Sensational violence dominated the news. A serial killer in Chicago strangled eight student nurses in their dormitory, and an ex-Marine climbed the university tower in Austin, Texas, to shoot thirty-five strangers. Grim stories also suffused popular culture, from Truman Capote's best-selling *In Cold Blood* to the gangster film *Bonnie and Clyde*: "They're young. They're in love. They kill people." All along, captured on film for television broadcasts, war came home from Vietnam. Weekly U.S. casualties reached 1,200 by January of 1967 and exceeded 2,000 before the end of March, with carnage tenfold higher for the Vietnamese.

Defying his entire senior staff, King agreed to address a large Vietnam protest rally at the United Nations Plaza in New York. The advisers warned of sectarian disaster, calling rally organizers "a squabbling, pacifist, socialist, hippie collection." Stokely Carmichael of SNCC, the main speaker, had become an ideological shooting star in the press. Black separatists expelled white staff members from SNCC, and Carmichael let Huey Newton of Oakland borrow his rural label from Alabama for gun-wielding Black Panthers of instant notoriety.

"I'm gonna march," King insisted. To cushion the risk, advisers arranged for him to declare his Vietnam stance first in a more controlled setting. John Bennett of Union Theological Seminary sponsored the event. Rabbi Abraham Heschel and historian Henry Steele Commager prepared commentary. On April 4, following a clerical procession into Riverside Church, King addressed an overflow crowd in the Gothic cathedral financed by John D. Rockefeller, Jr.

[From *At Canaan's Edge*, pp. 591–604]

A standing ovation died down to cavernous tension before King imposed deeper quiet with a meditation on hesitant voices. "I come to this magnificent house of worship tonight because my conscience leaves me no other choice," he said. Paying tribute to the first line of theologian Robert McAfee Brown's statement on Vietnam—"A time comes when silence is betrayal"—King confessed that the emotional vortex of war left doubters "mesmerized by uncertainty" and had made his pulpit "a vocation of agony" for the previous two years, "as I have moved to break the betrayal of my own silences and to speak from the burnings of my own heart." He still felt the forceful admonishment to leave Vietnam policy alone, King allowed, but it left him "nevertheless greatly saddened" that so many people considered the topic a senseless and disconnected shift from civil rights. That presumption fitted those who "have not really known me" or understood the movement, he lamented. "Indeed," said King, "their questions suggest that they do not know the world in which they live."

He undertook to explain "why I believe that the path from Dexter Avenue Baptist Church . . . leads clearly to this sanctuary tonight." Seven reasons began with two lesser ones confined to race. Vietnam had "broken and eviscerated" the historic momentum for justice since the bus boycott, he asserted. Moreover, circumstance compelled poor black soldiers to kill and die at nearly twice their proportion for a stated purpose to guarantee liberties in Southeast Asia that remained myths at home, fighting "in brutal solidarity" with white soldiers "for a nation that has been unable to seat them together in the same schools." King derived a third theme from young rioters who had countered his pleas for nonviolence with quips that the nation itself relied on "massive doses of violence" to solve social problems. "Their questions hit home," he intoned, "and I knew that I could never again raise my voice against the violence of the oppressed in the ghettos without having first spoken clearly to the greatest purveyor of violence in the world today—my own government."

This naked pronouncement further hushed Riverside as King moved through reasons centered in patriotism, his Nobel Prize commission, and religious imperative. Just as the movement always had adopted America's larger, defining goal of a more perfect democratic union—helping to spread concentric ripples of freedom behind rights for black people, liberating white Southerners themselves from segregation—so King argued by reverse synergy that a hardening climate of war could implode toward fearful subjugation at home. "If America's soul becomes totally poisoned," he warned, "part of the autopsy must read 'Vietnam.'" He marveled that religious leaders so readily evaded their core convictions to excuse violence. "Have they forgotten that my ministry is in obedience to the one who loved his enemies so fully that he died for them?" he asked. "What then can I say to the Vietcong, or to Castro, or to Mao, as a faithful minister of this one? Can I threaten them with death, or must I not share with them my life?" Finally, he declared for Vietnam an impetus broader than American ideals but short of religious apocalypse or perfection. "We are called upon to speak for the weak, for the voiceless, for the victims of our nation, for those it calls enemies," he said. "No document from human hands can make these humans any less our brothers."

King quickened his pace to describe decades of nearly continuous war from the viewpoint of ordinary Vietnamese. "They must see Americans as strange liberators," he said. His historical sketch grew relentlessly more intimate past the "tragic decision" of 1945 to revoke independence with a nine-year attempt to reestablish French colonial control. "Now they languish under our bombs," said King, "and consider us, not their fellow Vietnamese, their real enemies." He filtered out geopolitical labels to highlight personal realities on the ground. "They move sadly and apathetically as we herd them off the land of their fathers into concentration camps," said King. "They watch as we kill a million acres of their crops. . . . They wander into town and see thousands of the children homeless, without clothes, running in packs on the streets like animals." Villagers and soldiers degraded each other as Americans subjected their own troops to inner scars beyond the hazards of war. "We are adding cynicism to the process of death," he charged, "for they must know after a short period . . . that their government has sent them into a struggle among the Vietnamese. . . .

"Somehow this madness must cease," King declared, but he predicted no peace initiatives to match the appetite for war: "The world now demands a maturity of America that we may not be able to achieve." His audience stirred as from shock when he presented five proposals drawn from Allard Lowenstein's draft, including a permanent bombing halt and a unilateral cease-fire. Applause first greeted the final brisk point: "Five, set a date that we will remove all foreign troops from Vietnam in accordance with the 1954 Geneva Agreement." A renewed wave of approval swept over his immediate call for a national effort to "grant asylum to any Vietnamese who fears for his life under a new regime." King did not hide from the stigma of military defeat by Communists, nor quibble about negotiating terms. Yet neither did he discount anyone's yearning for democracy, whether a faceless peasant's or Lyndon Johnson's. Instead he offered bare, conflicted remorse for "sins and errors in Vietnam" that had neglected, spoiled, and trampled essential bonds of solidarity in freedom. By treating the Vietnamese more as subject "natives" than citizens, the American example long since undermined a democratic road to independence.

The Riverside crowd embraced King's message as though relieved to hear biting reflection sustained with nuance so devoid of malice, and perhaps also because his candid doubts of practical impact rang humbly true. They clapped for his endorsement of draft resistance and again for his praise of seventy declared conscientious objectors thus far from his Morehouse alma mater alone. He said each listener should weigh methods by individual conscience and collective promise—"But we must all protest." Witness to belief was more important than immediate results, he told them to more applause, "and if we ignore this sobering reality, we will find ourselves organizing Clergymen and Laymen Concerned committees for the next generation." The crowd stayed with King through skeins from his speeches since the Nobel Prize lecture. He called Vietnam symptomatic of a tragic impulse to meet rising hope in the world's "barefoot and shirtless people" with military force disguised as American values. "Communism is a judgment against our failure to make democracy real and follow through on the revolution that we initiated," he declared. Summoning a renewed freedom movement "out into a sometimes hostile world," seeking to overcome poverty, racism, and war, King's peroration ran past his text to extol again the biblical vision of the prophet Amos—"when justice will roll down like waters and righteousness like a mighty stream."

A second standing ovation gave way to hurried comments by the sponsors. . . . Among surprise well-wishers pushing through the throng came Morehouse schoolmate and Juilliard musician Robert Williams, who had composed his first published choral work, "I Can't Turn Back," one traumatized night during the bus boycott. From Riverside back to the Americana Hotel, Williams reclaimed his old Montgomery role as volunteer escort for a friend now euphoric with relief. Whatever happened, said King, the manifest attention to his speech meant that at least he was making plain to the world his brief for peace in Vietnam.

King first blamed distorted news coverage for a rude shock, which one historian called "almost universal condemnation" beyond the walls of Riverside. . . . "What on earth can Dr. King be talking about?" wrote a

Washington columnist on April 5, wondering how any civil rights leader could overlook the benefits of integrated combat. "If there hadn't been a war, it would have served the Negro cause well to start one." White House aides reacted strongly to King. Trusted counsel Harry McPherson warned President Johnson an hour before the Riverside event: "Martin Luther King has become the crown prince of the Vietniks." John Roche of Brandeis, who had succeeded Eric Goldman as Johnson's academic liaison, far outstripped McPherson's rare agitation the next day with a shrill judgment that King "has thrown in with the commies." In an "EYES ONLY" report to the President, Roche claimed inside knowledge that King, "who is inordinately ambitious and quite stupid (a bad combination) . . . is painting himself into a corner with a bunch of losers."

White House aide Clifford Alexander . . . and others mobilized civil rights leaders to isolate King's threat to their White House alliance. Former ambassador Carl Rowan angrily told King that millions of their fellow black people would suffer for his insults against the greatest civil rights president in American history . . . and King's folly became a front-page theme within a week of Riverside. "N.A.A.C.P. Decries Stand of Dr. King on Vietnam / Calls It a 'Serious Tactical Mistake' to Merge Rights and Peace Drives," announced the April 11 *New York Times.* . . .

Pressed for an admission that his peace talk did harm to Negroes, King lapsed into testiness that went unreported: "The war in Vietnam is a much graver injustice to Negroes than anything I could say against that war." After a speech at Occidental College, he kept telling advisers that the phalanx of rejection left him "temporarily at a loss." . . . He said even the White House aides half-apologized for their political offensive, complaining of war hawks on the other side. The only consolation King wrung from his plight was a dawning reminder of similar distress "in every movement we have started," and a night's reflection clarified the pattern. "This was very true in Birmingham," he told Levison. From President Kennedy on down, even nonsegregationists had opposed the disruption and protest, and no one had conceded any chance of a positive outcome. "The press was against me," said King. "The middle-class Negro community was against me, and finally they came around." The antiwar movement needed to fashion a breakthrough, like the children's marches or the confrontations on Pettus Bridge.

Levison cautioned against dangerous hopes. "It will be harder than Birmingham," he told King, which was disheartening indeed. Levison already conceded that the burden went deeper than specific words of the Riverside address or his own vanity as a speechwriter. American public discourse broadly denied King the standing to be heard on Vietnam at all. It invested mountains of calculation into military prospects but recoiled from any thought of withdrawal, especially on the recommendation of a civil rights preacher, and future generations would remain locked in what Andrew Young called debilitating paralysis between "those who are ashamed that we lost the war and those who are ashamed that we fought it."

King offered a precarious narrow course that demonized neither side, restrained by a nonviolent imperative to find slivers of humanity in the obscene polar conflict. While upholding for his own country, personified by Lyndon Johnson, a supreme but imperfect commitment to democratic norms, he granted the Vietnamese Communists a supreme but imperfect resolve to be free of external domination. On balance among Vietnamese, war by foreigners entrapped the complicit United States in a colonial past that forfeited liberating status. To curtail unspeakable cruelty and waste, Americans must refine their cherished idea of freedom by accepting that they could support but not impose it in Vietnam. To honor sacrifice with understanding, Americans must grant the Vietnamese people the elementary respect of citizens in disagreement. The lesson was at once wrenching and obvious, in the way modern people might be chastened by the centuries it took to establish that the Inquisition's bloody enforcement profaned rather than championed Christian belief.

King flew north to San Francisco, still stung. He complained most of featured editorials in two nationally eminent newspapers, the *Washington Post* and the *New York Times*, respectively a supporter and a critic of the war. While neither paper engaged the substance of his Riverside argument, both archly told him to leave Vietnam alone for his own sake. "Many who have listened to him with respect will never again accord him the same confidence," declared the *Post*. "He has diminished his usefulness to his cause, to his country, and to his people." Editors at the *Times* pronounced race relations difficult enough without his "wasteful and self-defeating" diversions into foreign affairs. In "Dr. King's Error," they summarized the Riverside speech as "a fusing of two public problems that are distinct and separate," and predicted that his initiative "could very well be disastrous for both causes.". . .

In Atlanta King ran into his neighbor Vincent Harding, the Spelman professor who had drafted most of the Riverside speech, and teased him for causing a month of ceaseless trouble. He complained of having to fight suggestions at every stop that his Vietnam stance merely echoed the vanguard buzz of Stokely Carmichael. Harding sensed Carmichael was swept up by a peculiarly American phenomenon in the mold of Malcolm X, built on the sensational illusion that violence alone measures power and that menacing language accordingly registers heroic strength rather than noise. Having devoted himself to Mennonite peace theology since his own military service in Korea, Harding still believed as a mentor that Carmichael and peers had been not only stronger through SNCC's formative era but also more "radical" in the true sense of going to root causes and solutions for injustice. King kept trying to reach SNCC veterans on precisely this point, stressing the bonds of common experience in the South. He startled Carmichael with a personal call near midnight on April 29, fairly begging him to attend church for once at Ebenezer the next morning.

With Carmichael seated in a front pew, King apologized for the rare use of a manuscript. His sermon embellished recent Vietnam speeches with confessions on the cumulative burden of nonviolence. He acknowledged resentment that history's victims remained so accountable for the overall state of race relations, still obliged to catalyze progress by further suffering and improvisation, and he bridled like Malcolm X that America admired nonviolence mostly when practiced by blacks for the comfort of whites. "They applauded us on the freedom rides when we accepted blows without retaliation," King declared with an edge of sarcasm. "They praised us in Albany and Birmingham and Selma, Alabama. Oh, the press was so noble in its applause and so noble in its praise that I was saying be nonviolent toward Bull Connor." His trademark passion, while quivering to defend a steady course, let slip rage at being patronized and misunderstood: "There is something strangely inconsistent about a nation and a press that will praise you when you say be nonviolent toward Jim Clark, but will curse you and damn you when you say be nonviolent toward little brown Vietnamese children!" The congregation broke into applause. "There is something wrong with that!"

Late in 1967, imprisoned retroactively by order of the U.S. Supreme Court, King would design a poor peoples' movement modeled on the 1934 Bonus March of World War I veterans. His cell mate, Rev. Wyatt Tee Walker, took this photograph with a camera smuggled into the Birmingham jail.

— CHAPTER SEVENTEEN —

Poverty: The Last Crusade, 1967–68

Historic cleavages divided politics during the fabled "Summer of Love," which was destined to represent the entire 1960s in caricature. That June, shortly before President Johnson appointed Thurgood Marshall to become its first black Justice, the Supreme Court in *Loving et Ux. v. Virginia* struck down the laws of sixteen states that criminalized interracial marriage. Simultaneously, in a 5–4 decision, the Court ordered Martin Luther King and seven fellow ministers back into the Birmingham jail, effective in October, to finish contempt sentences for violating local court orders that had forbidden them to protest segregation in 1963. A *New York Times* editorial, while regretting a penalty "embarrassing to the good name of the United States," approved the Court's signal that perennial unrest must give way to the rule of law.

Also in June of 1967, the Egyptian army marched across the Sinai Desert to join six Arab nations encircling Israel, bent upon annihilation, with a 25–1 advantage in population and a 3–1 superiority in war planes and tanks. Nevertheless, Israel astonished a breathless world with swift victory in the Six Day War. On June 7, when Israeli soldiers captured all of Jerusalem for the first time in 1,900 years, General Yitzhak Rabin vetoed a proposal to blow up both Muslim structures on the Temple Mount: Al Aksa Mosque and the Dome of the Rock. The war caused a sea change in world politics and Jewish identity. Pan-Arab nationalism dissolved. FBI wiretaps picked up Stanley Levison's premonition of waning intellectual support for nonviolence: "Half the peace movement is Jewish, and the Jews have all become hawks."

In July, huge riots caused catastrophic destruction in Newark and Detroit, which suffered nearly seventy deaths along with injuries and arrests in the thousands. King issued a doleful warning that any nation failing to provide jobs ultimately could not govern itself. President Johnson appointed Illinois Governor Otto Kerner to head a bipartisan study commission, whose conclusion would upset Johnson too much even to acknowledge its report: "White racism is essentially responsible for the explosive mixture which has been accumulating in our cities since the end of World War II."

In August, a National Mobilization Committee announced plans to converge on Washington for a giant demonstration against the Vietnam War. Flamboyant Yippie leaders vowed to exorcise or levitate the Pentagon. An unruly proliferation of Mobilization supporters dubbed the "New Left," largely from white college campuses, supplanted the press image of black protest from the sit-in era. In his upstart presidential campaign, targeting New Left elements as disloyal misfits and kooks, George Wallace deflected charges that he was the candidate of racial backlash. "I never made a statement in my political career that reflects on a man's race," he repeated indignantly. "My only interest is the restoration of local government."

Ever more isolated, King forged a new direction.

[From *At Canaan's Edge*, pp. 634–43, 648–56, 715–17]

President Johnson [made] harsh summer news on August 3. To curb inflation, and reduce a budget deficit projected to exceed $28 billion, he called for a 10 percent income tax surcharge. He also announced his decision to send another 55,000 soldiers to Vietnam, toward a new ceiling of 525,000 by mid-1968. The Pentagon request for 200,000 reinforcements remained officially secret, but a seminal *New York Times* story debunked the labored claim of slow victory only days later. It provoked Johnson enough to call the military press office in Saigon and denounce Communist influence behind the radioactive thesis, "Vietnam: The Signs of Stalemate." The President demanded action to root out commanders who disclosed to reporter R. W. Apple that they expected years more combat because enemy troop strength actually had increased despite thirty months of rising carnage: an estimated 200,000 enemy dead with 12,269 Americans killed and 74,818 wounded. On *Meet the Press*, meanwhile, correspondents pressed King to choose whether he would seek to revive nonviolent demonstrations against Vietnam or the race riots. They said colliding passions weakened either course. "The tragedy is that we are today engaged in two wars and we are losing both," King replied. "We are losing the war against poverty here at home. We are losing the war in Vietnam morally and politically.". . .

From a brisk overnight trip for *Meet the Press,* King returned home for the opening SCLC banquet on August 14 [1967]. Mayor Ivan Allen welcomed 1,400 guests to the ballroom of Atlanta's new Hyatt Regency Hotel. Aretha Franklin performed her hit songs "Respect" and "Baby I Love You," which shared the top of the current music charts with the Beatles' *Sgt. Pepper* album and Scott McKenzie's rhapsody on a flowering San Francisco youth movement. Actor Sidney Poitier described his pioneer screen roles since being stranded years ago on the "colored" side of the Atlanta bus station, and proclaimed King "a new man in an old world." Over three more days, Benjamin Spock addressed an overflow session on peace in Vietnam, and King explained to a heritage workshop that the convention's "Black Is Beautiful" posters signaled a drive to upgrade negative connotations buried deep in the English language. "They even tell us that a white lie is better than a black one," he said.

Delivering the annual president's report from his own pulpit, King recalled that when a handful of black preachers had gathered there at Ebenezer to form the Southern Christian Leadership Conference, just after the Montgomery bus boycott, such a glamorous banquet with three hundred white participants was scarcely conceivable. Libraries, white-collar jobs, and "the fresh air of public parks" had been off-limits to black people. Even casual association between races, when not illegal, was suffused with danger. "A decade ago, not a single Negro entered the legislative chambers of the South except as a porter or chauffeur," he said. To confront poverty and war above the stupendous legal achievements taking hold on the civil rights front, King called for renewed dedication to nonviolence. He waxed philosophical about a narrow path between anemic love and abusive power, preaching as though to himself on the trials of ministry in public service. "What I am trying to get you to see this morning is that a man may be self-centered in his self-denial and self-righteous in his self-sacrifice," King declared. "His generosity may feed his ego and his piety may feed his pride. So, without love, benevolence becomes egotism and martyrdom becomes spiritual pride.". . .

King's first attempt to set a course for nonviolent struggle collided with his headstrong inner circle. On Tuesday, September 12, [1967,] when SCLC's executive staff gathered at the Airlie House conference center in rural Virginia, James Bevel enjoyed a prodigal's welcome south after two years in Chicago and the peace movement, but celebrations turned into a strategic dispute. Folksinger Joan Baez favored a coordinated offensive to resist the war in Vietnam. She outlined her own preparations for pacifist demonstrations at military posts and conscription centers, protesting the coercion of young Americans to kill and be killed. In sharp contrast, the young lawyer Marian Wright championed a priority to uplift the invisible poor. She said that whereas the antiwar movement already had legions of recruits, national attention was turning away from people like her clients in Mississippi. She proposed to transport into Washington a representative host of faces from every region and race—men who never worked, women who could not read, children who seldom ate—for educational witness until Congress provided jobs or income. Wright modeled her notion on the Bonus Army of World War I veterans, who had occupied the capital to seek relief from the Great Depression.

Hosea Williams attacked both ideas. Civil rights had stalled over black power and urban riots beyond its Southern turf, he said, while even a stalwart black mother complained that "Dr. King went too far" to question foreign policy in wartime. Williams favored training new voters from the last great success at Selma, and still resented the reduction of his own Southwide staff from 180 fieldworkers to roughly a dozen. Bevel eloquently rebutted Williams, as usual. He argued that peace must be the first priority for any vanguard, prophetic movement, because Vietnam was devouring the spirit and treasure for any other national purpose. Jesse Jackson, Bevel's protégé, opposed either national drive before a catalyzing local success like Birmingham. For him, a move from weakness only invited humiliation. Jackson wanted first to rebuild SCLC's movement in heartland Chicago, where he said abundant numbers could be mobilized either for peace marches or the destitute poor.

King mostly listened. Abernathy and Young occasionally made favorable comments about a poverty caravan, but they reflected King's guarded wish rather than their own conviction. In fact, King alone had received Marian Wright's proposal like an answered prayer. Its focus on abject poverty opened an important but neglected dimension in human rights, where there was ample space for democratizing nonviolence outside the factional glare of the peace movement. Also, having been stumped about how to dramatize poverty from remote Mississippi or Alabama, King welcomed the inspiration to bring its faces and stories into the capital instead. Wright got the gist of her idea from [Senator] Robert Kennedy, who told her after the hearings in Mississippi that Congress would address such misery only if someone made it more uncomfortable not to.

Warring critiques elevated tension at Airlie House for five days. Historian Lawrence Reddick, King's first biographer, stalked out with a prickly declaration that he would hear no more grandiose plans while SCLC remained functionally incompetent and nearly bankrupt. When King tried a musical metaphor, imagining poverty harmonized in diverse strains from black and native Indian to Appalachian white, Joan Baez tartly questioned all that effort tuning an orchestra for slaughter in Vietnam. . . . To counter King's worry about surging hostilities that fragmented and discredited the Vietnam protest, Bevel belittled the poverty campaign as bus fare next to the crisis of a misguided war. He said the first duty of nonviolence was to resist organized brutality. If Washington and Jefferson risked "crucifixion" by kings to establish democracy, he preached, the lowliest American should do no less to refine the spirit and practice of equal citizenship. Late one night, King literally howled against the paralyzed debate. "I don't want to do this any more!" he shouted alone. "I want to go back to my little church!" He banged around and yelled, which summoned anxious friends outside his room until Young and Abernathy gently removed his whiskey and talked him to bed. King greeted colleagues sheepishly the next day. "Well, now it's established that I ain't a saint," he told newcomers before the retreat ended on Sunday, September 17. . . .

In public, meanwhile, King and Harry Belafonte launched an eight-city fund-raising tour that sorely disappointed their hopes to replenish the SCLC treasury. Audiences fell short, and performers even quarreled on stage. At the Oakland Coliseum, singer Sammy Davis warned a meager first-night crowd not to stray from traditional civil rights issues, and promoted his goodwill trip to entertain U.S. troops in Vietnam. Joan Baez promptly challenged Davis to beckon the soldiers home instead, winning mixed applause for her resolve to blockade the Army induction center nonviolently at dawn. As Baez stayed behind to serve ten days in jail with 123 fellow resisters, a bomb-threat evacuation delayed another small concert the next evening in Los Angeles. . . .

Almost unnoticed, King slipped into the aftershock of the Pentagon siege on Monday, October 23. His testimony before the Kerner Commission remained confidential, but it groped for anti-poverty tactics of "escalating nonviolence" somewhere between timid supplication and destructive riots. "Well," he told reporters outside, "I think that the time has come, if we can't get anything done otherwise, to camp right here in Washington just as they did with the Bonus March—just camp here and stay here by the thousands and thousands." These remarks, which the *Washington Post* called an "appeal to anarchy," earned no better public reception than his Washington concert with Belafonte and Aretha Franklin. . . . King's secretary, Dora McDonald, asked Levison to console King through a worrisome despondence over paltry crowds, and lawyer Chauncey Eskridge warned that the entire series "will be lucky to break even.". . .

[King] rushed home long enough to change into dungarees and return with three fellow defendants for an airport ceremony, on legal advice that they would become muted prisoners the moment they landed on Alabama soil. King told Atlanta reporters the sentence was "a small price to pay for the historic achievement" initiated in 1963 when "thousands of Negro citizens, facing dogs, fire hoses, mass arrests, and other outrages against human dignity, bore dramatic witness to the evils which pervaded in the most segregated city in our nation." At the same time, he cited the four dissenting Supreme Court Justices to excoriate the majority decision as churlish, vindictive, and dangerous. It was worse than jailing Boston patriots retroactively for dumping tea from Britain, because no theft or vandalism was at issue from the freedom marches. "As we leave for a Birmingham jail today," said King, "we call out to America: 'Take heed. Do not allow the Bill of Rights to become a prisoner of war.'"

Armed Alabama deputies, who boarded the departing flight with King's party, asserted control on arrival to wave wide-eyed regular passengers out of the airplane through a double line of officers forming in the rain. A hundred movement supporters waited in the Birmingham terminal to greet the four prisoners, only to watch them hauled off by police cars that darted onto the runway. Photographers captured King carrying three books to jail under his arm: the Bible, an economics text, and *The Confessions of Nat Turner*. A rare, two-part review in the *New York Times* had just praised William Styron's historical novel for bringing "coherent voice to a catastrophe we hardly knew had happened," but black critics faulted the author for projecting too glibly a writer's hold on inner thoughts from Nat Turner's bloody 1831 slave rebellion. "I absorbed by osmosis," Styron maintained, "a knowledge of what it is to be a Negro." . . .

With a smuggled camera, cell mate Wyatt Walker took a photograph of King staring through the bars. King complained of flu, and did not fulfill a notion to write a sequel for his Letter from Birmingham Jail. He made only tactical notes—including one for Harry Wachtel to reconvene at Union Seminary the fractious talks comparing Vietnam with the Six Day War in the Middle East—and he sketched a proposed "Bill of Rights for the Disadvantaged." His model was the 1944 GI Bill of Rights, and to a lesser degree the Bonus Act of 1936. The latter had passed over President Franklin Roosevelt's veto, reversing more than three years of sporadic government action to rout impoverished World War I veterans encamped in Washington. The GI Bill, which FDR passively and unhappily approved, helped transform the American economy with the offer of college tuition grants for 11 million World War II veterans. In jail, King began an opinion piece for the *New York Times*, arguing by analogy that the nation must take another leap of faith toward redress and opportunity. . . .

He vowed to lead a "camp-in" of poor people to Washington. "I'm on fire about the thing," King told seventy SCLC staff members at the Penn Conference Center in Frogmore, South Carolina. He said . . . they must rise above violent symptoms spreading from foreign war and domestic despair.

At the week-long retreat, beginning on November 26, he warned that only hysteria looked for rage to sustain idealism. "Violence has been the inseparable twin of materialism, the hallmark of its grandeur," he said. "This is the one thing about modern civilization that I do not want to imitate." He confided that he had just met with Olympic athletes trying to craft a protest of racism for the Mexico City Summer Games, only to find them disillusioned and abused by a black power conference at which delegates threatened to beat each other. Their ordeal underscored a lesson for King that "hate has no limits." He said, "I refuse to hate. Many of our inner conflicts are rooted in hate." King declared a moral imperative to dispel national hostility now clouding miracles from the civil rights movement. If resistance in Washington exceeded the travail of Birmingham or Selma, he pledged to intensify sacrifice accordingly. "So I say to you tonight that I have taken a vow," he announced at the retreat. "I, Martin Luther King, take thee, nonviolence, to be my wedded wife."

Bevel objected that no dramatic plunge could rescue a misguided strategy. Predicting that Americans would ignore the "camp-in," he argued that Vietnam rightly demanded the focused energy of a movement devoted to democratic values. . . . The poverty campaign stagnated all week in the Frogmore workshops. Only Bernard Lafayette, SCLC's new program director, pitched himself into the operational plans for his mandate, and Bill Rutherford, the new chief of staff, found the mood of the country distinctly unfavorable. ("Public preoccupation with Vietnam is stunning," he told Young.)

King worked from a blackboard, batting down objections. "The day of the demonstration isn't over," he said. "And I say to you that many of our confusions are dissolved—they are distilled in demonstrations." He denied that the campaign slogan, "Jobs or Income," was indecisive or inadequate. Their public goals had been simple in Birmingham and Selma, King insisted, and the program of Jesus himself boiled down to the word *repent.* "You see, I don't care if we don't name the demand," King declared. "Just *go* to Washington!" He said more than once that this might be the last campaign, because poverty was bigger than race. One of King's remarks— "the victory we seek, we'll never win"—provoked an eruption from Hosea

Williams that it was wrong to stir up vulnerable people for a losing battle. ("I got really upset," Williams recalled. "I just get cooking.") King pleaded with the staff not to shrink from lost causes or association with outcasts— "I would hope that we in SCLC are the custodians of hope"—in exhortations that rambled at times into distracted theology. "I'm not talking about some kind of superficial optimism which is little more than magic," said King. "I'm talking about that kind of hope that has an 'in spite of' quality." A distinctive rendition of one Bible verse* bubbled up: "There is something in the book of Revelation which says, 'Make an end on what you have left, even if it's near nothing.'"

King overrode doubt and dissent. He went straight home to a press conference on Monday, December 4—exactly eight months since taking on the furors of Vietnam at Riverside Church, one day before the twelfth anniversary of his debut speech for the bus boycott. Unlike the reluctant spokesman whose thunderclap oratory first caught up with Montgomery's local protest, now he conjured up a resurgence by sheer force of will. "The Southern Christian Leadership Conference will lead waves of the nation's poor and disinherited to Washington, DC, next spring," King announced. The campaign would begin with three thousand pilgrims "trained in the discipline of nonviolence," and last until the country responded. "We don't know what will happen," he declared. "They may try to run us out. They did it with the Bonus Marches years ago, you remember." Fielding questions about potential clashes, he vowed to desist only if the protesters themselves indulged in violence. "The Negro leader's mood seemed deeply pessimistic," reported the *New York Times*, and the front page heralded trouble: "Dr. King Planning to Disrupt Capital in Drive for Jobs."...

In tumultuous mid-March 1968, Martin Luther King quietly tested strategies to overcome social barriers by nonviolence, being far from sure they would work. He closed to reporters his anxious summit meeting with seventy-eight "non-black" minority leaders on Thursday, March 14. Mostly unknown to each other, let alone to King, they ventured by invitation from

---

* Apparently a paraphrase of Revelation 3:2: "Awake, and strengthen what remains and is on the point of death."

across the United States to Paschal's Motor Lodge in the heart of black Atlanta. Wallace Mad Bear Anderson spoke for a poor Iroquois confederation of upstate New York. A deputy came from the bedside of César Chávez, who had barely survived a twenty-five-day fast in penance for violent lapses by striking California farmworkers. Tillie Walker and Rose Crow Flies High represented plains tribes from North Dakota, while Dennis Banks led a delegation of Anishinabes. During introductions, Bernard Lafayette whispered to King what he had gleaned about basic differences among Puerto Ricans, as distinct from Mexicans (Chicanos), or the defining cause of the Assiniboin/Lakota leader Hank Adams, who spearheaded a drive for Northwestern salmon fishing rights under the 1854 Treaty of Medicine Creek. Lafayette had checked repeatedly to make sure King wanted the hardscrabble white groups, and the answer was always simple: "Are they poor?"

Paschal's was dotted with coal miners, some of whom braved fierce criticism from Appalachian rivals, and Peggy Terry admitted being raised in a Kentucky Klan family. After moving to Montgomery during the bus boycott, she had gone once on a lark to see "that smart aleck nigger come out of jail," and the actual sight of King buffeted by a mob churned into her independent nature. Now Terry sheltered a few black friends in the Jobs Or Income Now (JOIN) group from uptown Chicago's poor white district, and she wowed movement crowds by asking where else a hillbilly housewife could trade ideas or jail cells with a Nobel Prize winner.

Hosea Williams made no secret of his wish for the nonblack summit to fail. With several other SCLC staff leaders, he mercilessly ribbed young Tom Houck, who had come into the St. Augustine movement as an orphaned high school dropout from Massachusetts, then stayed on to chauffeur the Kings, and since had developed enough grit to scour the country for nonblack leaders under tutelage from Lafayette and Bill Rutherford. "First he was Coretta's boy," groused Williams. "Now he's taking our money and giving it to Indians." Internal staff resistance complained that these strangers would slow them down, ruin cohesion, and make it even tougher to compete with the black power trend. Lafayette fretted constantly over the risk of insult to, from, and between the guests. Leaders did rise from the floor to complain of exclusion, but they also acknowledged initiatives adapted from the black movement. Since the bus boycott, said several Native Americans, the model tribal leader no longer was an "Uncle Tomahawk" angling for token promotion. Others questioned nonviolence with doubtful respect. Vincent Harding, who had drafted most of the Riverside Vietnam speech, came late to observe and made note of hushed deliberation on assorted faces contemplating whether to recommend the experimental coalition under King.

In an aside, King first asked, "Tijerina who?" He absorbed a fiery speech about regaining communal lands stolen by noncompliance with the Treaty of Guadalupe Hidalgo, in which the United States had acquired the territory that became seven Southwestern states to end the Mexican-American War of 1848. Lafayette cautioned that Reies López Tijerina was a charismatic, chronic fugitive—hailed as a Chicano Malcolm X, disparaged as a "wetback" Don Quixote—best known for leading an armed protest posse that briefly occupied a New Mexico courthouse on June 5, 1967. At Paschal's, Tijerina asked what mention of land issues would be offered in return for nonviolent discipline, and King said the answer flowed from the movement's nature: a common willingness to sacrifice put all their grievances on equal footing. On reflection, Tijerina proposed that particular stories from Native American groups be dramatized first in Washington, followed by black people second and his own Spanish-speaking groups last. His offer, which deferred both to historical order and the spirit of King's presentation, received acclamation that extended to Chicano leaders sometimes at odds with Tijerina, such as Corky González of Denver. The summit closed on a wave of immense relief. Myles Horton, who helped recruit the white Appalachians, expressed euphoria after nearly four decades of cross-cultural isolation at his Highlander Folk School. "I believe we caught a glimpse of the future," he told Andrew Young.

Striking sanitation workers picket under armored guard in downtown Memphis.

— CHAPTER EIGHTEEN —

Requiem in Memphis, 1968

King dragged recalcitrant staff members into preparations for the poverty campaign. His valued counselor James Lawson, then pastoring a church in Memphis, had warned that years of trauma had reduced some aides to chronic fatigue, dissipation, or worse. Rival factions accused James Bevel and Hosea Williams of plotting to usurp King's place. Jesse Jackson waxed independent.

King pushed on through barnstorming recruitments in primitive rural churches. A mother came forward in Marks, Mississippi, to say her children ate pinto beans "morning noon and night." Another said hers stayed home from school because they had no clothes. Ralph Abernathy and Andrew Young were surprised to see tears roll down King's face. Resolving to start the poverty mule train from Marks, he recounted searing testimonies by name at Jennings Temple Church in Greenwood that night, less than two years since the Meredith march. "I wept with them," King confessed. ". . . And we are going to say in no uncertain terms that we aren't going to accept it any longer. We've got to go to Washington in big numbers."

Yet another detour intervened. Tracked down by phone, King yielded to a plea from Lawson to support a strike for union recognition by sanitation workers in Memphis. During a severe thunderstorm, because of city rules against their seeking shelter in residential areas, two "tub men" had crammed into a truck's rear cylinder and been crushed accidentally by the pistonlike compactor meant for garbage. This event precipitated a walkout with a special slogan to assert humanity in the honor of the lost employees, Echol Cole and Robert Walker: "I AM A MAN." On March 18, with Lawson, King addressed a rousing crowd of 15,000 at the vast Mason Temple. Inspired by an embattled struggle so imbued with his national purpose, King offered to return.

As always, he kept crisscrossing the country to fuel his movement. From Hattiesburg and Bessemer, King flew on March 25 to New York's Catskill Mountains for the 68th Rabbinical Assembly of conservative Jews. There he described a bond with his host, Rabbi Abraham Heschel, grounded in the latter's teaching that the prophetic doctrine of equal souls before God prefigured the democratic ideal of equal votes. King fielded questions about separatism and "anti-Israel Negroes." He said Israel needed security just as displaced Arabs needed opportunity, and that violence would secure neither. Heschel saluted King, asking, "Where in America today do we hear a voice like the voice of the prophets of Israel?" He solicited pledges for the poverty campaign, and the rabbis sang "We Shall Overcome" in Hebrew.

From Atlanta on March 28, delayed by bomb threats, King arrived late to the head of a teeming march into downtown Memphis. Almost immediately, behind a thousand sanitation workers, roving black teenagers darted from the ranks to break store windows. Noise and sirens spread panic. Lawson and his marshals herded a retreat by bullhorn as aides pushed King into a passing car. A police lieutenant guided them behind roadblocks to a nearby inn.

[From *At Canaan's Edge*, pp. 734–39, 755–66]

The violence in Memphis was a godsend to the FBI," wrote King scholar Adam Fairclough. Until then, under intense pressure from headquarters, the field offices churned out operations against King mostly aimed for harassment or sabotage. When SCLC sent out fundraising letters to seventy thousand supporters late in March, headquarters approved a fictitious news leak to Northern newspapers that King did not need contributions because Washington churches and synagogues already had agreed to support the poverty marchers. Headquarters simultaneously authorized anonymous letters to selected black outlets in the South stating just the opposite—there was "no provision to house or feed marchers" in a Washington campaign geared for "King's personal aggrandizement." (Director Hoover issued the usual security instructions: "Prepare the letters on commercially purchased stationery and take all necessary precautions to insure they cannot be traced to the Bureau.") Otherwise, the schemes ran to propaganda. . . .

FBI headquarters seized upon the Memphis upheaval within hours. Top officials disseminated to "cooperative news sources" a blind memorandum stating that "the result of King's famous espousal of nonviolence was vandalism, looting, and riot." The lapse from nonviolent discipline freed the FBI from inhibitions due to public respect for King's conduct, if not his message, which opened character assassination on all fronts, and by the next day, March 29, Hoover approved a second effort "to publicize hypocrisy on the part of Martin Luther King." The document whiplashed him as cowardly and violent, servile and uppity. "Like Judas leading lambs to slaughter," Hoover confidentially advised news contacts, "King led the marchers to violence, and when the violence broke out, King disappeared." A gossipy addition highlighted the place of refuge. "The fine Hotel Lorraine in Memphis is owned and patronized exclusively by Negroes," stated the propaganda sheet, but King had chosen instead "the plush Holiday Inn Motel, white owned, operated, and almost exclusively white patronized." This petty account twisted every motive and circumstance to release torrents of FBI contempt. By April 2, Hoover formally requested permission to reinstall wiretaps at SCLC. Two days later, the Mississippi FBI office sent headquarters a two-pronged COINTELPRO proposal, first, to breed confusion and resentment on King's poverty tours by spreading false information about whether he or surrogates would appear at scheduled rallies, and second, to distribute leaflets skewering King as a fancy dresser who deserted his people. The combination would "discredit King and his aides with poor Negroes who he is seeking support from," argued Mississippi, but the Bureau would not have time to act on the plan. . . .

King called Stanley Levison with thanks for encouragement on points that had sustained him through the press conference, then relapsed into fears of ruin. He said influential black critics scented his weakness over this—Roy Wilkins, Bayard Rustin, Adam Clayton Powell—and would reinforce the public damage. "You know, their point is, 'Martin Luther King is dead, he's finished,'" King complained. " 'His nonviolence is nothing. No one is listening to it.' Let's face it. We do have a great public relations setback."

"That is only if you accept their definition," Levison replied, "and this, I think, is a profound error you are making."

No, King insisted. The problem was widespread eagerness to see things that way. "I talked to the fellows who organized the violence business this morning in my room," he said. "They came to me. I didn't even call for them. They came up here—they love me. They were fighting the leadership of Memphis. They were fighting Jim Lawson. . . . They were too sick to see that what they were doing yesterday was hurting me much more than it could hurt the local preachers. But it is out now. What do we do?" He said he was thinking of extremes such as one of Gandhi's long fasts for penance.

"Martin, I'm not just talking about this march," Levison persisted. "I'm talking in general about what seems to me the box or the trap that you are placing nonviolence in. The other side can always find a few provocateurs to start violence no matter what you do." King would be paralyzed unless he could "hypnotize every single Negro alive," said Levison. "That's too much to ask."

King, like James Lawson, said the movement was distorted by unstable myths in the press. For years, stories suggested that most American black people accepted nonviolence, when in fact only a tiny fraction practiced its severe leadership discipline. Then stories perceived a massive shift from the presumed weakness of "Negro nonviolence" to the projected virility of black power, although even tinier numbers accepted political violence. Still, King told Levison he was in no position to correct false impressions now that a riot "broke out right in the ranks of our march." He could not go to Washington promising only one percent violence, and therefore he must seek rehabilitation in Memphis. "So I've got to do something that becomes a kind of powerful act," he said. Until then, he would be dismissed. . . .

Tornado warnings [on April 3] made King fret about his crowd, as ominous streaks of gray and purple crossed the sky from the west. Radio bulletins told of a seven o'clock twister that picked up and dumped a stretch of asphalt on cars near Star City, Arkansas, killing seven people, and the first squalls hit Memphis half an hour later in slanted sheets of rain. Phone calls from the Lorraine to Lawson in Mason Temple verified that the crowd indeed was thin—perhaps fewer than two thousand in the huge hall that had packed seven times that many for King's visit on March 18. . . .

King came smiling to the microphones about 9:30, just as the storms crested. (Tornadoes killed five more people. One at ten o'clock demolished forty trailer homes just north of Memphis, where the only serious injury was a man struck by a flying television.) He strung together several of his speech themes aimed toward the shared moment, beginning with a poetical tour of history. "If I were standing at the beginning of time," and could choose any lifetime, he would "take my mental flight" past the glories of ancient Egypt, Greece, and Rome—"But I wouldn't stop there," he kept saying—down past scenes from the Renaissance and Martin Luther and Abraham Lincoln until he could say, "If you allow me to live just a few years in the second half of the twentieth century, I will be happy." It might seem strange with the world so messed up, King said, but he chose above all to see the stirrings of a human rights revolution for freedom worldwide. . . .

He saluted every aspect of the Memphis movement, beginning with the families of sanitation workers. . . . Abruptly King swerved into a third oratorical run, retelling of his brush with death when a demented woman stabbed him at a Harlem bookstore in 1958—how a doctor told the *New York Times* that the blade would have severed his aorta if he so much as sneezed, and how a little girl wrote a simple letter of thanks that he did not sneeze. "I want to say that I am happy that I didn't sneeze," said King, "because if I had sneezed, I wouldn't have been around here in 1960 when students all over the South started sitting in at lunch counters. And I knew that as they were sitting in, they were really standing up for the best in the American dream, and taking the whole nation back to those great wells of democracy. . . ." His voice climbed again in rhythm and fervor, using survival as a melodramatic device to relive the civil rights movement. "If I had sneezed," he cried near the end, "I wouldn't have been down in Selma."

Experienced preachers behind him felt fleeting anxiety that King might miss his landing, because he was in full passion on a peroration unsuited to close. The "sneeze" run always came earlier in his speeches, being informal and thin. King sputtered at the podium, then slipped a gear. "And they were telling me—now it doesn't matter now," he said. "It really doesn't matter. I left Atlanta this morning. . . ." He told briskly of the pilot's bomb search announcement. "And then I got into Memphis." He frowned. "And some began to say the threats—or talk about the threats—that were out, what would happen to me from some of our sick white brothers. Well, I don't *know* what will happen now. We've got some difficult days ahead. But it doesn't matter with me now."

King paused. "Because I've been to the mountaintop," he declared in a trembling voice. Cheers and applause erupted. Some people jerked involuntarily to their feet, and others rose slowly like a choir. "And I don't mind," he said, trailing off beneath the second and third waves of response. "Like anybody I would like to live—a long life—longevity has its place." The whole building suddenly hushed, which let sounds of thunder and rain fall from the roof. "But I'm not concerned about that now," said King. "I just want to do God's will." There was a subdued call of "Yes!" in the crowd. "And he's allowed me to go up the mountain," King cried, building intensity. "And I've looked over. And I have s-e-e-e-e-e-n the promised land." His voice searched a long peak over the word "seen," then hesitated and landed with quick relief on "the promised land," as though discovering a friend. He stared out over the microphones with brimming eyes and the trace of a smile. "And I may not get there with you," he shouted, "but I want you to *know, tonight* ["Yes!"] that we as a people will get to the promised land!" He stared again over the claps and cries, while the preachers closed toward him from behind. "So I'm happy tonight!" rushed King. "I'm not worried about *any*thing! I'm not fearing *any* man! Mine eyes have seen the *glo*-ry of the coming of the Lord!" He broke off the quotation and stumbled sideways into a hug from Abernathy. The preachers helped him to a chair, some crying, and tumult washed through the Mason Temple.

King sat spent, drenched in perspiration. Friends gathered around with congratulations and wonder for his thunderclap ending of little more than one hundred words. They said he transcended death while capturing freedom, gazing forward and backward on both. They compared details from the biblical story of Moses, who was permitted to see Canaan across the Jordan River from atop Mount Nebo, but died there for transgressions before his people entered the Promised Land. King revived in preacher talk with peers, and lingered eagerly to greet the sanitation workers. Notwithstanding an endless day since the airport bomb search, in fact, he hummed with incandescent stamina and disappeared with Abernathy and Bernard Lee for a long night on the town. . . .

By mid-afternoon, as the last major witness in the federal hearing on whether to permit or enjoin a renewed march, Andrew Young withstood withering cross-examination on "the so-called doctrine of nonviolence," which lawyers for Memphis treated like a crackpot myth. "Now the nonviolent school is to be distinguished from the so-called passive school?" asked one, who wondered how meek notions could be squared with militant words. Young managed to parry a question about how the movement had "plagued" Birmingham in 1963. "Really, by marching down to City Hall every day for about forty-five days," he said, "and having a prayer meeting." He did concede that he had never seen King so depressed by the difficulty of maintaining nonviolent discipline and spirit. . . .

"I would like to remind you that there is almost no place else in the world where people even assume that this kind of change should come about nonviolently except Martin Luther King and the Southern Leadership Conference. There is no tradition of nonviolence anywhere else in the world, in labor, and even in most areas of our own government," Young testified in a rush. "And certainly when America felt oppressed by Britain, they didn't seek nonviolence to seek redress of grievance. So I say we do have probably the only vested interest in nonviolence in this society, and we intend to make it work, and we would not want to run any unnecessary risks, because it jeopardizes what Dr. King has made a way of life for him."

The lawyer for Memphis suffered the outburst. "Are you through?" he asked.

"Yes, sir," said Young.

At four o'clock . . . an escaped convict bought a pair of Bushnell binoculars just up Main Street at York Arms Company, one of the businesses whose windows were smashed on March 28. He drove back to finish setting up a surveillance post. . . . The convict had driven from Atlanta, where the newspapers said King was leaving for a march in Memphis, arriving late the previous night. This day, reading front-page news that King was staying at the Lorraine, and perhaps hearing radio reports that specified Room 306, he had located and studied the motel until an hour ago, when he rented a room for $8.50 per week in Bessie Brewer's flophouse next door to Fire Station Number 2. With the seven-power Bushnells, he could read room numbers on the motel doors seventy yards distant, and the same strength on his Redfield scope would make human figures seem only thirty feet away. The scope was mounted on a .30-06 Remington Gamemaster, which was engineered so that its 150-grain slug would lose less than .01 inch in altitude and reach the motel balcony with 2,370 pounds of knockdown power—enough to drop a rhinoceros. However, the odd angle of an occluding building next door meant the convict could fire the long rifle only by leaning out his window. To avoid that, he must wait until he sighted his target from the room, then run with the rifle down the hallway to the common bathroom, find it unoccupied, and hope King stayed long enough on the balcony to get a clear shot from a rear window above the bathtub.

About five o'clock, when Andrew Young returned from court to find a general bull session, King greeted him with playful fury by wrestling him to the floor between the two beds. Abernathy, Hosea Williams, Bernard Lee, and A. D. King joined in a wild tickling punishment of Young for failure to keep "our Leader" informed all day, which turned into a free-for-all pillow fight, with King sometimes squaring off against his younger brother A. D. as in childhood. Once the hysteria subsided, Young said he thought the hearing went pretty well. Chauncey Eskridge walked in from a lawyers' conference with U.S. District Judge Bailey Brown just as the motel television shifted from local news centered on last night's tornadoes ("death and destruction . . . over the mid-South last night") to the network broadcast. King joked that his esteemed lawyer was more reliable even than Walter Cronkite, and Eskridge said Judge Brown would permit SCLC to lead Monday's march under the restrictions King and Lawson desired: a prescribed route, no weapons, and narrow ranks to give the marshals wide space on the flanks to keep the spectators away. This relief started a fresh buzz of determination for weekend preparations. Young claimed vindication. . . .

They should all get ready for dinner, King said, and a police surveillance officer noted through binoculars at 5:40 his brisk walk with Abernathy upstairs to their Room 306.

While dressing, Abernathy disclosed sheepishly to King that he could not join him in Washington for the preliminary lobbying in the Poor People's Campaign, because the new start date of April 29 conflicted with his long-scheduled spring revival in Atlanta. King said this would never do. West Hunter Street Baptist was a magnificent congregation, he purred, claiming that he would have gone there himself if Daddy King had not invited him to Ebenezer, and surely the deacons would understand that Abernathy had to revive the soul of a whole nation instead. Abernathy weakened, but did not give in until King promised to help secure a substitute revival leader of stature. He placed a call to a New Orleans revivalist. In the esoteric bargaining, King and Abernathy used the little-known childhood first names they reserved for each other in private—Michael and David, respectively—and they ignored the commotion outside. Upstairs, Hosea Williams loudly evicted the last of the semi-penitent young rioters from two rooms provided during negotiations, after discovering to his outrage that fifteen of them had crammed inside to live on meals charged to the SCLC account. Downstairs, Jesse Jackson rehearsed an Operation Breadbasket ensemble, and bystanders crowded into the room to belt out extra hymns such as "Yield Not to Temptation" and "I'm So Glad Trouble Don't Last Always."

Rev. Billy Kyles left Jackson's songfest and knocked at Room 306 to hurry King along. Abernathy played him for a sign of deliverance. "Why don't you do my revival?" he asked Kyles, who adroitly dodged, saying he thought he was scheduled to preach in Columbus, Ohio. King chimed in to needle Kyles about the relative status of his invitations. "Anybody'd rather come to Atlanta than go to Columbus," he said. He shifted tone to inquire how Memphis churches achieved such unity behind the sanitation workers, who were not members of the prestige congregations, but Abernathy reopened preachers' banter on the subject of food. "All right now Billy, I don't want you fooling me," he said, warning that if he went all the way to the Kyleses' home for T-bone steaks or filet mignons, which he pronounced "FEEL-ay MEEN-yuns," then, "you're gonna flunk." King shuddered at the memory of a preacher in Atlanta whose house was so big that he could afford to serve only cold ham bone, cold potatoes, cold bread, and Kool-Aid. Abernathy said the Kool-Aid wasn't even sweet.

"Now Billy," said King, "if you've bought this big new house and can't afford to feed us, I'm gonna tell everybody in the country."

Kyles rejoined that there would be more soul food than King's waistline needed.

"Your wife can't cook, anyway," King teased. "She's too good-looking." He fell into a chauvinist bromide about the value of plain wives, and Abernathy took up the flip side with remarks on the beauty of Gwen Kyles. He retreated to the bathroom with a flirtatious grin that he must splash on Aramis cologne just for her.

King walked ahead of Kyles to look over the handrail outside, down on a bustling scene in the parking lot. Police undercover agent Marrell McCullough parked almost directly below, returning with King's aides James Orange and James Bevel from a shopping trip to buy overalls. Orange unfolded his massive frame from McCullough's little blue Volkswagen, tussling with Bevel, and Andrew Young stepped up to rescue Bevel by shadow-boxing at a distance. King called down benignly from the floor above for Orange to be careful with preachers half his size. McCullough and Orange walked back to talk with two female college students who pulled in just behind them. Jesse Jackson emerged from the rehearsal room, which reminded King to extend his rapprochement. "Jesse, I want you to come to dinner with me," he said.

Kyles, overhearing on his way down the balcony stairs, told King not to worry because Jackson already had secured his own invitation. Abernathy shouted from Room 306 for King to make sure Jackson did not try to bring his whole Breadbasket band, while Chauncey Eskridge was telling Jackson he should upgrade from turtleneck to necktie for dinner. Jackson called up to King: "Doc, you remember Ben Branch?" He said Breadbasket's lead saxophonist and song leader was a native of Memphis.

"Oh yes, he's my man," said King. "How are you, Ben?" Branch waved. King recalled his signature number from Chicago. "Ben, make sure you play 'Precious Lord, Take My Hand,' in the meeting tonight," he called down. "Play it real pretty."

"Okay, Doc, I will."

Solomon Jones, the volunteer chauffeur, called up to bring coats for a chilly night. There was no reply. Extended time on the balcony had turned lethal, which left hanging the last words fixed on a gospel song of refuge. King stood still for once, and his sojourn on earth went blank.

Looking Back, and Ahead

[From *Parting the Waters* (1988), pp. xi–xii.]

Almost as color defines vision itself, race shapes the cultural eye—what we do and do not notice, the reach of empathy and the alignment of response. This subliminal force recommends care in choosing a point of view for a history grounded in race. Strictly speaking, this book is not a biography of Martin Luther King, Jr., though he is at its heart. To re-create the perceptions within his inherited world would isolate most readers, including myself, far outside familiar boundaries. But to focus upon the historical King, as generally established by his impact on white society, would exclude much of the texture of his life, which I believe makes for unstable history and collapsible myth. . . .

My purpose is to write a history of the civil rights movement out of the conviction from which it was made, namely that truth requires a maximum effort to see through the eyes of strangers, foreigners, and enemies. I hope to sustain my theses that King's life is the best and most important metaphor for American history in the watershed postwar years.

[From *Pillar of Fire* (1998), pp. xiii, 611–13]

There was no historical precedent for Birmingham, Alabama, in April and May of 1963, when the power balance of a great nation turned not on clashing armies or global commerce but on the youngest student demonstrators of African descent, down to first- and second-graders. Only the literature of Passover ascribes such impact to the fate of minors, and never before was a country transformed, arguably redeemed, by the active moral witness of schoolchildren.

The miracle of Birmingham might have stood alone as the culmination of a freedom movement grown slowly out of Southern black churches. Yet it was merely the strongest of many tides that crested in the movement's peak years, 1963–65. They challenged, inspired, and confounded America over the meaning of simple words: dignity, equal votes, equal souls. They gripped Malcolm X along with President Johnson, buffeted the watchwords "integration" and "nonviolence," broke bodies and spirits, enlarged freedom. . . .

In 1976, Bob Moses returned from Africa after a decade in exile. After his last SNCC meeting in February of 1965, as Bob Parris, he had drifted from Mississippi into Alabama following the marches from Selma to Montgomery, when Martin Luther King had brought Abraham Heschel down to stay with him in Selma, with James Bevel sleeping in a bathtub and James Forman under the dining room table, and the rabbi surviving a garlanded march beside King, saying, "I felt like I was praying with my feet." Sometimes movement friends came across Parris on rural farms, drinking corn whiskey out of a fruit jar, thinking about the war in Southeast Asia. He attended the first organized protest on April 17, 1965. "Use Mississippi not as a moral lightning rod," he told a crowd of 15,000 at the Washington Monument, "but if you use it at all, use it as your looking glass.". . .

Parris, feeling invisible, decided it was safe to become Moses again. His marriage collapsed, partly over his obsession with Vietnam, just before he received a military induction notice. At thirty-one, beyond legal draft age, Moses interpreted the order as punishment for his statements against the war. He fled underground to Canada in August of 1966, living under the assumed name Robinson. . . . When he reached Tanzania that summer [of 1968], Moses turned in his false passport to the Tanzanian government, which granted him tacit asylum under his own name. He married Janet Jemmott, a SNCC worker he had met during Freedom Summer, and they had four children while teaching math and English, respectively, in a Tanzanian village school. . . .

After the Vietnam War ended, the Moses-Jemmott family returned to the United States and settled under the Jimmy Carter draft amnesty in Cambridge, Massachusetts. Janet Jemmott went to medical school and became a pediatrician. Moses taught high school and went back to graduate school at Harvard. He seemed disconnected from his past, even fearful of it. Some friends counted him among the many "movement casualties" haunted or damaged to varying degrees. He avoided SNCC reunions at which some of the survivors came to terms. Diane Nash told her peers at one of them that, to her own amazement, the late 1960s had swept away even her belief in nonviolence. "I felt that way for a few years until I noticed that I hadn't killed anybody," she said. "I hadn't even been to the rifle range. I hadn't blown up anything, and truly, I had done very little." Nash had disengaged under cover of words, she said, perhaps the better to raise children as a divorced single mother.

In 1982, Moses returned to Mississippi for the first time in sixteen years, to attend Amzie Moore's funeral. He made a brief speech. He began to give interviews, and sometimes he asked for documents about himself as though discovering another person. He developed a new way of teaching algebra that blended Freedom School methods. By the 1990s, his Algebra Project operated in school districts across the country. Moses spent more and more time in Mississippi, having recovered his past. Mastering first-year algebra is an equivalent of the right to vote in the 1960s, he said. It provides hope in the modern world.

[From *At Canaan's Edge* (2006), pp. xi, 769–71]

N onviolence is an orphan among democratic ideas. It has nearly vanished from public discourse even though the most basic element of free government—the vote—has no other meaning. Every ballot is a piece of nonviolence, signifying hard-won consent to raise politics above firepower and bloody conquest. Such compacts work more or less securely in different lands. Nations can gain strength from vote-based institutions to uphold commerce and civil society, but the whole architecture of representative democracy springs from the handiwork of nonviolence.

America's Founders centered political responsibility in the citizens themselves, but, nearly two centuries later, no one expected a largely invisible and dependent racial minority to ignite protests of steadfast courage—boycotts, sit-ins, Freedom Rides, jail marches—dramatized by stunning forbearance and equilibrium into the jaws of hatred. During the short career of Martin Luther King, Jr., between 1954 and 1968, the nonviolent civil rights movement lifted the patriotic spirit of the United States toward our defining national purpose. . . .

Shortly after the assassination, over wiretapped phone lines, a grief-stricken Stanley Levison complained that most Americans already distorted the loss of their "plaster saint who was going to protect them from angry Negroes." Pride and fear subverted King's legacy from all sides. James Bevel, ignoring the frailty of life, promptly declared King's killer James Earl Ray a mere pawn, because "there is no way a ten-cent white boy could develop a plan to kill a million-dollar black man." In 1978, Bevel stood witness at an eerie wedding ceremony conducted in prison by James Lawson, helping Ray begin his short-lived marriage to a courtroom artist. More than forgiveness, the motive of Bevel and Lawson was to assert that some evil greater than Ray must account for all the pain, and some casualties from the movement gave way to the undertow of many conspiracies. . . . Dexter King publicly proclaimed James Earl Ray innocent of his father's murder in 1997—"in a strange sort of way, we're both victims"—citing fantastic theories grounded in dogma that the federal government was guilty instead.

Critics of the movement made political history from a mirror distrust. In 1983, President Reagan announced his belief that secret FBI files one day would establish whether King was a loyal American or a Communist sympathizer. "But since they seem bent on making it [King's birthday] a national holiday," he added, "I believe the symbolism of that day is important enough that I will sign that legislation when it reaches my desk." Reagan's sunny disposition tempered his political platform that government was bad—proven despotic, incompetent, and wasteful—at least when aimed toward the purposes of the civil rights era. This became the dominant idea in American politics, as a cyclical adjustment in history shifted the emphasis of patriotic language from citizenship to consumer complaint, shrinking the public space.

A paradox remains. Statecraft is still preoccupied with the levers of spies and force, even though two centuries of increasingly lethal "total war" since Napoleon suggest a diminishing power of violence to sustain governance in the modern world. Military leaders themselves often stress the political limits of warfare, but politics is slow to recognize the glaring impact of nonviolent power. In 1987, students spilling into the streets of South Korea compelled a dictator to respect a permanent structure for elections. In 1989, the Soviet empire suddenly dissolved in a velvet revolution of dockworkers' strikes and choruses of "We Shall Overcome" at the dismantled Berlin Wall. There was no warning from experts, nor any hint of the nuclear cataclysm long prepared for and dreaded. That same year, Chinese students inspired the world from Tiananmen Square with nonviolent demonstrations modeled on the sit-ins, planting seeds of democracy in the authoritarian shell of Communist control. In 1990, Nelson Mandela emerged from twenty-seven years in prison to a Cape Town balcony, where he destroyed the iron rule of apartheid not with Armageddon's revenge but a plea for hopeful consent: "Universal suffrage on a common voters' roll in a united, democratic, and non-racial South Africa is the only way to peace and racial harmony."

Like America's original Founders, those who marched for civil rights reduced power to human scale. They invested enormous hope in the capacity of ordinary people to create bonds of citizenship based on simple ideals—"We the people"—and in a sturdy design to balance self-government with public trust. They projected freedom as America's only story in a harsh world. "The arc of the moral universe is long," King often said, quoting the abolitionist Theodore Parker, "but it bends toward justice." His oratory mined twin doctrines of equal souls and equal votes in the common ground of nonviolence, and justice refined history until its fires dimmed for a time.

King himself upheld nonviolence until he was nearly alone among colleagues weary of sacrifice. To the end, he resisted incitements to violence, cynicism, and tribal retreat. He grasped freedom seen and unseen, rooted in ecumenical faith, sustaining patriotism to brighten the heritage of his country for all people. These treasures abide with lasting promise from America in the King years.

Acknowledgments

There is no need to list again the multitude of research institutions and sources cited individually in the underlying trilogy, *America in the King Years*. However, I do want to repeat my indebtedness to them. This short history, like the narrative from which most of it is drawn, rests on the painstaking work of many archivists who have gathered materials essential for informed scholarship and debate. Also, to hundreds of participants and witnesses identified in the earlier books, I renew my heartfelt thanks for discussing memories and arguments from all sides of the civil rights struggle. The transcripts and digitally preserved recordings of those interviews, plus voluminous supporting files, are deposited under my name for public use at the Southern Historical Collection of the University of North Carolina Library in Chapel Hill.

Many catalysts sparked this single-volume adaptation. I appreciate thoughtful encouragement from Lesley Herrmann and Lance Warren of the Gilder Lehrman Institute of American History in New York. For decades, their foundation has been distributing primary materials to enliven the presentation of history in schools, and they have sponsored discussions for me with teachers and students across the United States. Jim Cameron of Saline, Michigan, led effective workshops on pedagogy in the digital age, and I am especially grateful for tutelage from Bill Schiess at Madison High School in Rexburg, Idaho. On the college level, audiences and seminars over many years have provided valuable criticism on ways to sharpen and sustain historical interest among new readers. Most recently, as Visiting Honors Professor at Chapel Hill in the spring of 2012, I learned a great deal not only from my co-teacher, Dr. James Leloudis, but also from seventeen insightful students who devoured my entire trilogy among several other texts in a single semester.

This book would not exist without my publishers at Simon & Schuster. That is a truism, of course, but I want to express thanks for assistance beyond the norm. Publisher Jonathan Karp fostered innovation. A large team shepherded the book toward publication. Many of them are familiar and reassuring to me from work together on previous books: Fred Chase, Jonathan Evans, Irene Kheradi, Julia Prosser, and Jackie Seow. Others are new colleagues: Richard Rhorer, Rachelle Andujar, Karyn Marcus, Jonathan Cox, Joy O'Meara, and photo researcher Jody Potter. I thank them all.

Finally, there are several people so close that it is hard to thank them adequately in public. Liz Darhansoff, my literary agent, has shared fellowship and summer refuge along with skillful guidance through a publishing industry in transition. Alice Mayhew, my chosen editor, remains an anchor through this our seventh joint book project—not counting one we discreetly set aside in the early 1970s. My wife, Christy, seasons our private devotion with her professional calling at the International Youth Foundation. Her mother has just turned 100, nurtured still by her garden, and our children Macy and Franklin are well launched into a troubled world. I am grateful for them, for concentric friends at every stage, and for the hopeful pleasures of the written word.

—Taylor Branch, May 2012

Index

Photo Credits